MIDWEST FRONTIER STORIES
- Collection 1

A treasury of first hand stories in original wording by the frontier settlers of the Midwest about the period of 1815-1845.
 (Primarily South East Iowa and North East Missouri)

- FIRST EDITION -

Compiled and edited by
Ed Scharff and
Leila Scharff

Cover Photo Courtesy of
Sky Shepard Images

"Sod House in Woods"
Wesley Woods of Indianola, Iowa

Midwest Frontier Stories – Collection 1
Copyright © 2017 by Ed and Leila Scharff

All rights reserved. No part of this book may be reproduced or transmitted in any form or by any means without written permission from the author.

ISBN-13   9780999494509
ISBN-10   0999494503
Library of Congress Control Number: 2017916914

Website: www.midwestfrontierstories.com

Manufactured in the United States of America

Dedication

Midwest Frontier Stories - Collection 1
Is dedicated to Giles Oldham Sullivan, Grandson of Capt. James Sullivan who with George Rogers Clark is credited with capturing Kaskaskia (1778) and Vincennes (1779) from the British during the Revolutionary War and securing the Old Northwest for the United States.

Giles was one of the first settlers in the territory that became Iowa:
1797 born in Louisville, KY;
1808 moved to St. Louis, MO;
1815 cattle Drive to Canada
(as far as sand prairie north of Des Moines River);
1821 Daughter born north of Des Moines River;
18?? independent Scout for Gen Dodge;
1827 Corporal in Winnebago War;
1830 settled near St Francisville, MO;
1833 trading post at Nashville, IA;
1835 first settler and founder of Bentonsport, IA;
1839 moved to Robertson Colony Milam Co, Texas;
1849-50 believe killed by the Comanche Indians.

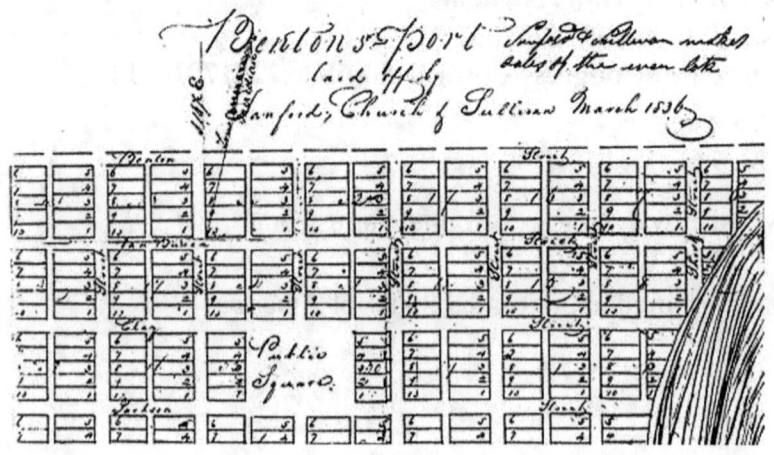

Preface

During years of personal genealogical research, we have uncovered fun documentation hidden in small libraries around the Midwest. Since most of them could not be scanned to OCR, we felt it our duty to create this anthology of first-hand and eye-witness accounts, or stories, written by the first settlers of Wisconsin and Iowa Territory.

Bear in mind the time these stories were written about. Almost nothing of today's world existed, no roads or bridges, only the flintlock gun (which was useless in damp weather), no percussion caps, rifles, or revolvers. For the most part, the Indian was a friend and neighbor. Settlements were along rivers and streams, transportation was mainly by dugout canoe, on foot or horseback, and yet they traveled long distances and apparently frequently.

These stories have been selected to give a good understanding of the life of the early frontier settlers of the Midwest. They may or may not be 100% accurate, but definitely give insight into the time.

Most stories are **un-altered** from their original wording, archaic word spellings, grammar, paragraphing and punctuation have been retained. Notes have been added to aid the reader in understanding the articles and archaic words.

Many stories contain genealogical data that is almost never found, such as hair and eye color, body build, distinguishing features, character, birth location and movement upon the frontier.

The 1836 Ledger of Sweet home shows some of the settlers in the area. As best we could, we have identified pictures of some of the settlers in this book. Please let us know if they are incorrect!

We hope you enjoy learning about the Old (mid)WEST as much as we have.

Sincerely,

Ed and Leila Scharff

Special gratitude to
- **Missouri and Iowa State archives**
- **Iowa Libraries: Keokuk, Burlington, Montrose, Dubuque and Fort Madison**
- **Missouri Libraries: Kahoka, Palmyra, St Louis County and St. Charles.**
- **Roger McPherson and Mike Miller for sharing the 1836 ledger of Sweet Home, MO.**

Table of Contents

Construction Techniques in the 1830's 1
Those Blessed Mice 5
Old Peg Horns 11
Comment on Old Peg Horns 14
Buffalo in 1820 15
Wedding of Thirty-Five Years Ago 17
West Point Lot Sales 9/10/1836 23
A Typical Iowa Cabin & Free Mail Delivery 29
Incidents of the Early Days in Keokuk 31
1815 Cattle drive from St. Louis, MO to Canada 35
Overland in 1870 41
Keokuk Under the Hill 47

Early Iowa Indians 53
   Origin of the name Devil Creek 55
   Mr. Reed's account of Black Hawk 59
   Black Hawk as an Elder 67
   How the Indians Counted and Pioneer Life 69
   The Great Indian Battle of Iowaville 71
   Comments on the Indian Battle at Iowaville 87
   Horrible Indian Depredations in Iowa 91
   More Indian Hostilities! 99

FIRST SETTLERS OF VAN BUREN COUNTY 101
   James Alfrey 101
   William Nelson 103
   Richard M. Jones 104
   Abel Galland 104
   A. W. Harlan 108
   Captain James White 112
   Ansons – Frank, George & Henry 115
   Peter Gillis 115
   Elijah Purdom 115

David A. Ely 116
Giles Sullivan 116
Winnena Sullivan 118
Samuel C. Reid 119
Shapley P. Ross 120
Willcock 120
Nowell 121
Abiatha Buck Williams 123

SETTLEMENT OF DES MOINES VALLEY 131
Wm. Meek 131
Isham Keith 133
Thomas Blankenship 134
Charles Gaston 135
Joseph Perkins 135
Isaac Reid 135
Isaac Bird 138
William Fallis 138
James Blankenship 138
Mr Patchett 144
James Jenkins 144
Edward L. Longwell 145
Meashack Sigler 146

Glossary: i

Definition of Indian Words and Names v

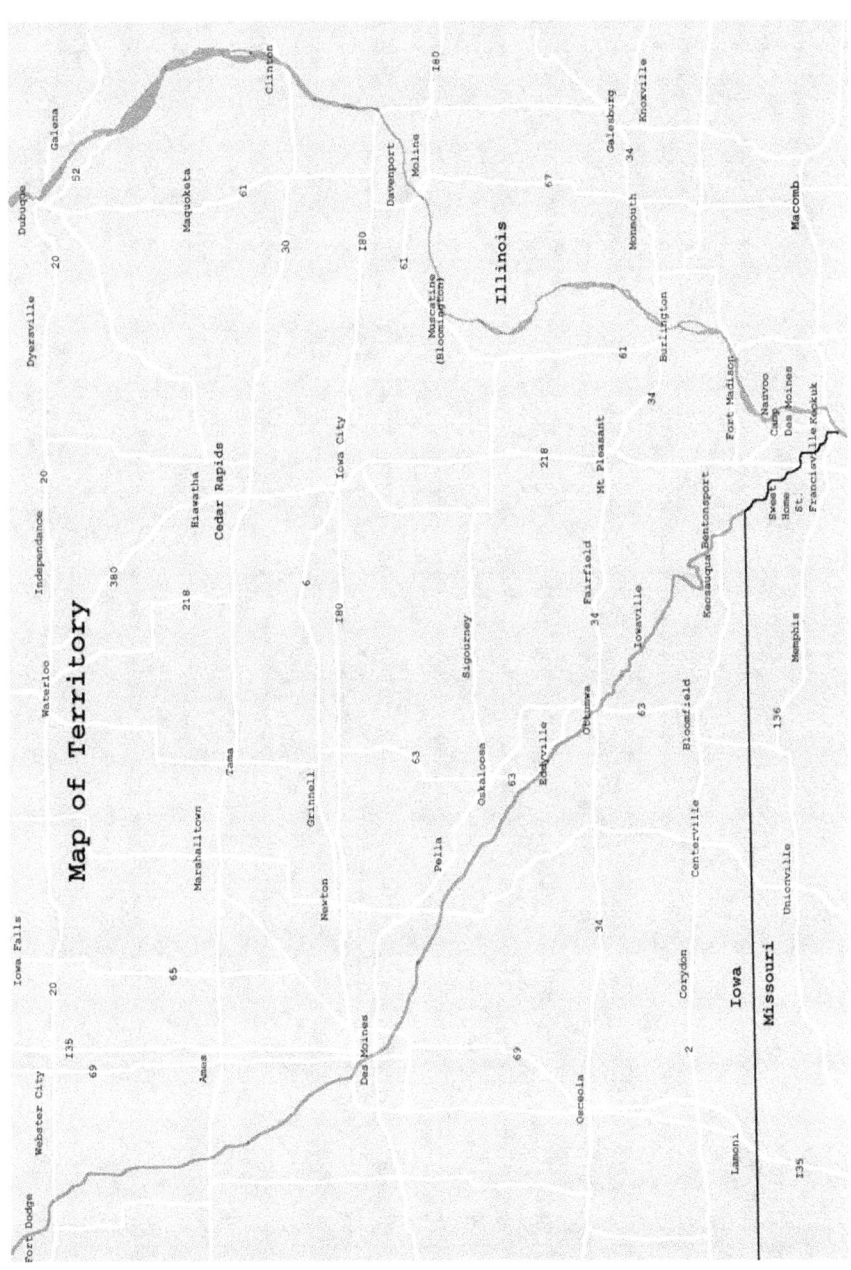

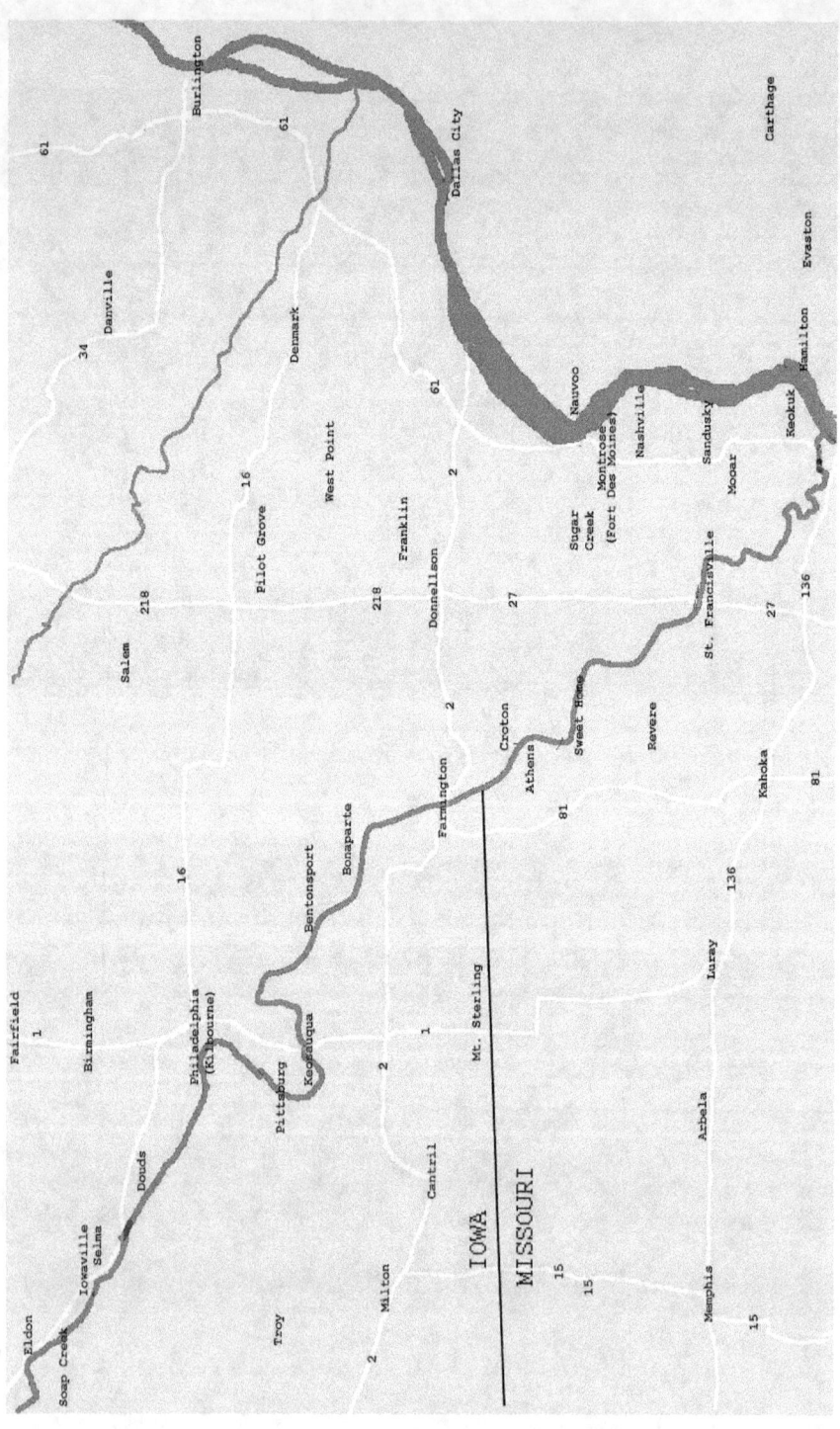

Construction Techniques in the 1830's

This description of life in the 1830's appeared in the February 5th 1899 issue of "The Gate City" of Keokuk Iowa. Note: How happy they were with a simple life, limited food selection and few possessions.

In the construction of our log houses no nail or sound of the hammer was heard. The wooden pin was our sole reliance. So used to the pin had we become, wagon-makers pinned the spokes into the hub. So honest and faithful was this done that we have worked three or four hours to free a hub of its spokes. Little capital was tied up in wagons - a sled would do us in the mud or for what little snow fell in our region; in dry weather a truck would do, made entirely of wood; not an ounce of iron was invested or used on it. For motive power we used oxen largely - their yokes of the present pattern, with a ring and staple of hickory. We often used the oxen to plow, both single and double. We have seen an ox hitched to a plow and all the harness, from the clevis to the collar, made of hickory withes[1] except the back band; that was rawhide.

---

[1] tough flexible branch of willow to bind or wrap

Our schools were taught in deserted houses temporarily repaired for the purpose. The seats were benches without backs and all of the same height for young and old. If a child's legs were not long enough for his feet to reach the floor they could dangle in midair.

If we raised wheat we threshed it sometimes with the flail[2], but usually by tramping it out with horses or oxen. We chose an elevated spot of ground where the water could run off if it rained, set a post down, pinned a light piece of wood five or six feet long loosely so it would revolve, hitched a pair of horses or oxen to the outer end, covered the floor with bundles and went to threshing. When we were through

---

[2] a threshing tool consisting of a wooden staff with a short heavy stick swinging from it.

threshing we cleaned out most of the straw, waited for a good wind, took it little at a time, mounted a box and poured it down before the wind. Thus we cleaned our grain.

Our traveling was done either on horseback or with horse and oxen team. The wagon was a clumsy affair, with the tread six inches wider than is used at the present time. The tongue[3] was twelve feet long. Instead of the neck yoke, chains reached from the end of the tongue back to the harness. The tongue and harness were fastened together - no joint as at present. When the wagon was idle, careful men propped up the tongue with forked sticks to keep it from sagging. If the near forward wheel struck an obstruction the near horse got a sock-dolger[4], sometimes nearly knocking him off his feet; ditto for the left wheel. Of roads we had none worthy of the name. We had wagon tracks upon which people traveled. The coach carried what little mail there was used then. When any part of the road became gullied[5] out or a tree fell across it, we made a new track.

We were a patient and satisfied people with our "hog and hominy," Lindsay[6] Pantaloons[7], warmers[8] for winter and a tow[9] change for summer. We were as happy and contented as a half-starved colt on the sunny side of a hay stack on a warm day in April.

We can't prove that a republican policy was the cause of waking us up from this stupid loafing slavery lethargy. We can prove they both came together and that the democrats fought every inch of progress from the time of the revival until now, are at it today as zealous as they were forty years ago.

---

[3] Long board attached to the front of the wagon to pull and steer it
[4] a forceful blow (from the other wheel)
[5] eroded ravine in soil from the tracks
[6] Coarse woven linen
[7] Tight fitting pants to show muscularity of legs
[8] Tight fitting jacket to keep warm
[9] Clothing made from the coarse, broken fibre, removed during processing flax, hemp, or jute

The awakening began in 1854; the Democrats took the do-nothing side except in the case of slavery. When it was in danger they were alert with all their weapons in good order. When pension, homestead, river and harbor and tariff laws were discussed, then they seized the constitution and O my! but they did larrup[10] the Republicans for breaking it. They have been the custodians of the constitution since Calhoun, father of the party, taught them how to use it

---

[10] to beat or thrash

Those Blessed Mice

This surprising story of survival in 1831 was written by A.W. Harlan and appeared in "The Daily Gate City" on Nov. 26, 1870

"Those Blessed Mice" would answer for a text for Henry Ward Beecher. It was only a by-word here in 1834, and for some years after that date. And thereby hangs a tale that I shall now try to relate, as I heard the circumstances given by one of the party, with due allowances for what I may have forgotten in thirty-six years.

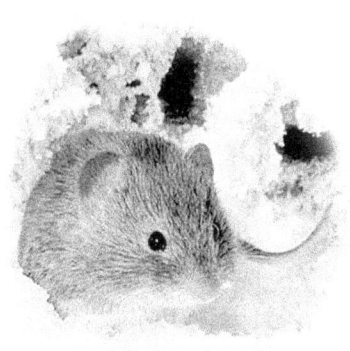

In the fall of 1831, the year before the Black Hawk war, Dr. Isaac Galland, Peter Williams and two or three other persons had been to Galena, Illinois, and went on to the west side of the Mississippi on a prospecting tour in the Vicinity of where Dubuque is now situated; but at that time it was Black Hawk's hunting ground, on which but few white men ventured.

The reader will bear in mind that up to this time all the travel to and from the lead mines about Galena was done on the Illinois side of the river.

But the little party of whom I am writing concluded that they would go home down on the west side of the Mississippi. The Indians were not very friendly to white men generally, but Dr. Galland had many personal friends among them, and as they carried no arms they concluded to make the venture.

They carried their camp equipage[11] with them without any extra pack horses. Their stock of provisions was rather light, but as it was early in October, they thought in case of emergency that

---

[11] Equipment or supplies, especially military ones

they could cross over at Rock Island to get some additional supplies; but when they got opposite Rock Island, at that time a United States military Post, the ice was running very heavy, and no soldier would volunteer to go over to them, so they kept on down the river. The weather was cold, but as yet no snow.

But not far from Flint Hills - say a few miles above where Burlington is now situated - a snow storm come on them, and in one day and night it fell to the depth of two and a half feet deep, and they were truly in a dilemma. Heretofore their horses could get something to eat, but could get nothing now but the bark of trees. The party had but one small axe or tomahawk with which to cut brush for their horses, but then they had nothing but elm bark on which to feed themselves.

The reader will observe that I have left a space to be filled by his own reflections. What the private thoughts of the several members of the party were I never learned, but they did not despair. They mounted their horses and pushed on to Flint Hills, hoping to find an Indian Camp. There were no Indians there as yet. They had been snowed in, and had not time as yet to return from their fall hunt.

The small party moved on down, crossed Skunk River without any serious difficulty, horses and men nearly exhausted. Here they had hoped to have found some Indians, but there was not even any Indian sign nor any tracks of game of any kind; and even if a deer had appeared in sight, it would only have been an additional vexation, as they had no gun.

The wind began to blow, the trees squeaked, and the weather became much colder. There was not even a prospect that the coons would stir for a month or two.

(A pause for thinking)

Dr. Galland told them if they could only hold out to reach a certain point, about a mile and a half below Fort Madison, that he knew the exact spot where the Indians had made a cache[12] or buried some corn under the ground.

---

[12] hiding place for stores of food or supplies

They took up the line of march in single file, breaking a path through the snow, and when the horse in front would become exhausted the next would take the lead, and the one that had been in front would fall in the rear. Thus they silently worked their tedious way, and a little before sunset reached the designated place, and hurried into a cottonwood grove near by. While some kindled a fire and prepared camp, the Doctor and some one else was hunting for the cache.

Most persons are aware how a deep snow will sometimes change the appearance of familiar places. The Doctor could not determine the exact spot at which the corn was buried and so reported to the others at the campfire.

The reader must fill the above space with his own reflections, while I state the exact position. The men and horses had been for two days and nights exerting themselves severely with noting to eat but elm bark. The evening was cold, and getting colder. The wind whistled dismally through the cottonwood tops. Here they were almost in sight of their homes neither horse or man could have moved two miles further. But those men were men who had camped out before this time.

One more effort must be made. Someone else would go with the Doctor. They went and searched long. At last they found several trails of mice, mostly centering in one place. This raised their hopes. They scratched away the snow, dug in the earth, and at last reached that precious store of corn. The horses were fed sparingly.

Some corn was put in a camp kettle and was soon boiling. Some blankets were placed so as to partially shield them from the wind and the social chat around the campfire was again resumed, but in rather subdued tones. The corn was boiling, it became soft; the men took a few grains at a time, and ate slowly for a time, and after the expiration of near two horses each made a moderate meal on boiled corn alone. Then they become comfortable and rather quiet - talked in rather subdued tones and all laid hushed. Peter Williams broke the silence by observing in a solemn tone, "Was it not them blessed mice that showed us the way to the corn?"

My first visit to this same spot was about three years from the time of the above occurrence, then again in January, 1835, at which time the snow was nearly two feet deep. The first settler near the place was by the name of Kennedy. Nathaniel Knapp and Old Dick Cheney lived where Fort Madison was and is yet. Then there was one settler out near Sugar Creek whose name was Wilson. Three companies of the 1st U.S. Dragoons were in garrison at Camp Des Moines, now Montrose. This was all. A death like stillness prevailed at this vast expanse of country lay in its primeval glory covered with a sheet of snow near two feet deep.

I shall now try to add some additional facts that may be of some interest to the man of a reflective mind.

Then again, twenty years or more had elapsed in which only I passed this place once until last fall, viz[13]: 1869, making in all near 35 years. I stopped, looked all around me - how changed the scene. Those thousands of acres are nearly all in cultivation, subdivided into fruitful fields. Nauvoo, Illinois, is in sight, where within a few years a vast swarm of fanatics have settled, built a city, a splendid Temple, introduced all the appliances of civilization, and have been expelled, their city has vanished, and the Temple is nearly all removed. Other fanatics have occupied their places, planted their vineyards, ate their fruits and are dispersing.

As I stood on a sand ridge below Fort Madison last Fall, trying to determine certain localities, the changes of 35 years were unrolled before me like a panorama. I could look back and see Black Hawk's band moving up Devil Creek, their squaws with papooses in a wooden frame lashed onto their backs, but today the locomotive is puffing over the same ground at wonderful

---

[13] Namely, in other words

speed, with sumptuous sleeping cars attached, and telegraph near by.

Then I looked to the hill sides. Much of the original forest land disappeared, the apple orchard and vineyard having taken their places. Again I contemplated this wonderful change - all changed in thirty-five years, save only the Father of Waters still rolled by with undiminished volume. The hum of a busy city was just in hearing. A strange sound caught my ear. I listened again. It was the heavy thug, thug of the trip hammers in the Penitentiary, and I waked up again.

Now let me close this sketch by informing the reader that I have forgotten the names of the other parties composing that little squad that felt thankful for boiled corn. Peter Williams some years after was living in Illinois, some two or three miles above Nauvoo, and I have neither seen nor heard from him for many years.

As for Dr. Isaac Galland, he was a man of extraordinary natural abilities, with a limited education, and when I first saw him, in 1834, must have been over forty years of age, and then as gray as a rat. His early life had been one combined scene of turmoil, strife and reckless adventure. I have heard him tell of scenes through which he had passed, one of which turned his hair gray in a single night. I shall not relate any of these adventures. Let them rest with the past. But after the Black Hawk war he was comparatively a quiet man. True, he had something to do is buying up Half-Breed lands; something to do with the Mormons and the laying off of Zarahemla, near where Montrose is at present; has been a party to some few suits relative to Half-Breed lands, occasionally bandied[14] a few personal epithets[15] with certain members of the Lee County Bar. He went to California in about 1853, returned about 1856. He felt old age creeping on him. He settled just below Fort Madison and there

---

[14] pass on or discuss (an idea or rumor) in a casual or uninformed way.
[15] an adjective or descriptive phrase expressing a quality characteristic of the person or thing mentioned.

ended his days some few years ago near the same place where tracks of those blessed mice showed them the way to the corn.

Notwithstanding the Doctor's industry and good natural abilities, he began to realize in his old age that his life was a failure. He became rather petulant; would get quite angry at small offences; then woe unto the luckless Wight[16] on whom he attempted to ventilate his vocabulary of abusive epithets.

---

[16] A living creature, especially a human being

Old Peg Horns
the Pioneer Cow of the Des Moines Valley

This life and travels of the pioneer cow "Old Peg Horns" was printed in "The Daily Gate City" on Nov. 12, 1870. The extinct Alderney breed originated on Alderney Island of the British Channel, said to be smaller and more deer like than bovine. "The Alderney ranks as the best butter cow in the world, whilst its abundant yield of milk, rich in cream, is phenomenal"-1912

Peg Horns was a sucking calf in 1809, not far from where the town of Brookville, Indiana, is now situated. That was almost three years before the last British war. John Phillips owned her mother, who was a family favorite. Said John Phillips emigrated to Ten-Mile Creek, near Fort Clark, now Peoria, Illinois, at an early day. At his place old Billy Clark, who is still living near me in Clark County, Missouri, became acquainted with her in 1824. Peg Horns was at that time only fifteen years old.

Then said John Phillips emigrated to the lead mines in 1828, taking Peg Horns along with him, and remained about two years near Galena, Illinois. Then again, about the year 1830, said John Phillips came on to the Rapids, and crossed over to Mexico Point, now known as Nashville, in Lee County, Iowa. He remained about one year, and then moved over to Missouri, taking his stock of cattle with him - most of them descended from Old Peg Horns. He settled near Jerry Wayland, where is now the town of St. Francisville, Missouri. Here Phillips thought of settling. There was at that time a great range for stock, and Dr. Trabue had a tread mill on Honey Creek, that was within ten miles of him. This was a convenience that he had not been used to for many years.

In the fall of 1831 winter set in more than a month earlier than usual, and proved the severest ever known. In February, 1832, the great ice freshet[17] came. Let me try to describe. The ice was very heavy, even for the Des Moines River, say from one to two feet thick. The cut-off at the island was but partly made. Here the ice first started to run, and commenced gorging at the lower end of the cut-off, and become stationary; and as the ice would break loose above it would run down on to the first gorge and run up the stationary ice, thus rendering it still more immovable. The river was rising rapidly; the ice crowded down until it overflowed the banks and filled in amongst the timber; then it broke over the bank at Wayland's place and took down through the prairie next the sand ridge, and as the water would spread on the prairie it at first became shallower, thus letting the ice stop on the prairie, and soon it all become a vast ice gorge in many places about St. Francisville, being from 10 to 15 feet deep in the timber, and thus it continued to gorge on up to Bentonsport.

---

[17] spring thaw of river or stream when breaking ice can block the stream and cause deadly flooding along the stream or river. Sometimes called an Ice Jam or Ice Dam.

During most of this time Phillips cattle - that is old Peg Horns and her family- were swimming around in the timber above the island. But old Peg Horns seemed to be aware that the whole surface of the earth was not likely to be flooded again, so she led the way to the sand ridge, the others following. About one-half of them reached terra firma, the balance died by the way.

The distance that they must have worried through this ice was all of a half mile, and the only strange thing about the matter was that any of them reached land. But old Peg Horns made the riffle[18], and took a new lease of life.

After Phillips had lost most of his cattle he concluded this was rather a poor, cold country, so he sold his cattle or most of them to old Samuel Hearn, and went to Texas.

I do not remember whether Bill Phelps bought Peg Horns of John Phillips or Samuel Hearn. The first time I saw her was at Sweet Home, MO, in the fall of 1834, and at that time she must have been twenty-four or twenty-five years old. No one disputed her age after looking at her horns. I will not boast of her fine appearance, for I have seen many better looking cows in appearance. She bore a stronger resemblance to the Alderney[19] stock than she did to Durhams[20]. I am aware that there has been many good milch[21] cows in the west; almost every pioneer family have had their favorite, but old Peg Horns was a gem among the favorite milkers; the quantity was fair; the quality most excellent, and then she was always on hand at milking time, and never kicked the pail over. She never was inclined to run away or lay out of nights. True, after raising more than twenty calves and seeing none of her progeny about her she concluded to quit raising calves, but she did not quit giving milk, and wherever Bill Phelps moved, old Peg Horns went as one of the family, and he moved almost every year, as all the Indian traders did. Peg Horns seemed to know she had a pretty good master. Phelps knew she

---

[18] shallow stream with rapid current, surface broken by rocks
[19] The Alderney breed was similar to the Guernsey, but much smaller and considered extinct.
[20] Breed that today is called shorthorn
[21] Middle English word for milk giving, also German in origin.

was one of the best of milch cows. The last time that I saw her was at Fort Sanford, near Agency City, in 1842. She was then about thirty-three years old, and still a good cow; had been giving milk more than seven years without having a calf. When Bill Phelps left the Des Moines, in 1844, I did hear that he gave Old Peg Horns to some friend of his, so I never heard of her dying.

This is a tolerable tall cow story, and if any antiquarian wishes further items, they can inquire of old Samuel Hearn, in Keokuk, of Jeremiah Wayland and George Haywood, at St. Francisville, Missouri, or of Mrs. Nancy Bedell, Jo. J. Benning, Mrs. Susan Benning, or old Billy Clark, of Athens, Missouri.

Comment on Old Peg Horns

A follow up comment on the article about Old Peg Horns written by someone who calls themselves Iron Clad was Printed in "The Daily Gate City" on Nov. 17, 1870

Having come to this State when, it was thinly settled, and after reading Col. Harlan's writings, I have no doubt of the truth of every word he writes, and I would be glad if I had such a memory. He in his last communication speaks of Bill Phelps often as an old pioneer. When I was a boy I boarded with old Bill at Des Moines Agency, in 1845, and found the old man very pleasant in every respect. Many incidents happened there that it is not necessary to relate. My friend Harlan writes about Old Bill Phelps, and his cow, "Peg Horns," but he don't tell all the facts, as I am informed that when old Bill left for Des Moines or "Raccoon Forks," as used to call it, he started old Peg Horns up the Des Moines River, and held to her tail, and she brought him to Des Moines in less than twenty-four hours, from near Mr. Harlan's residence, where he lives now. I am informed by the parties, if Mr. H. wants to prove the facts - Tom Colwell, Jo. J. Benning and Old Billy Clark, all of Clark county, MO, and friends of old Bill - that he sill lives in Illinois, and looks as young as he did twenty-five years ago.

However that was a mighty old cow and good for milk and was also a good swimmer.

Buffalo in 1820

A reprint of the Dubuque Times story describing buffalo in 1820 near Dubuque appeared in the 4/10/1872 issue of "The Daily Gate City"

Fifty-two years ago, Iowa swarmed with buffaloes. An "Old Settler" tells the Dubuque Times that "as a contrast between fifty years ago and now, it may be said that Captain Morgan, with a few dragoons, passed across Iowa from Council Bluffs to the hills five miles west of Dubuque, in 1820.

There he beheld what is now Dubuque city and Julian Township, covered with so many thousands of buffaloes passing southward, that he remained in camp three days before daring to venture on his journey."

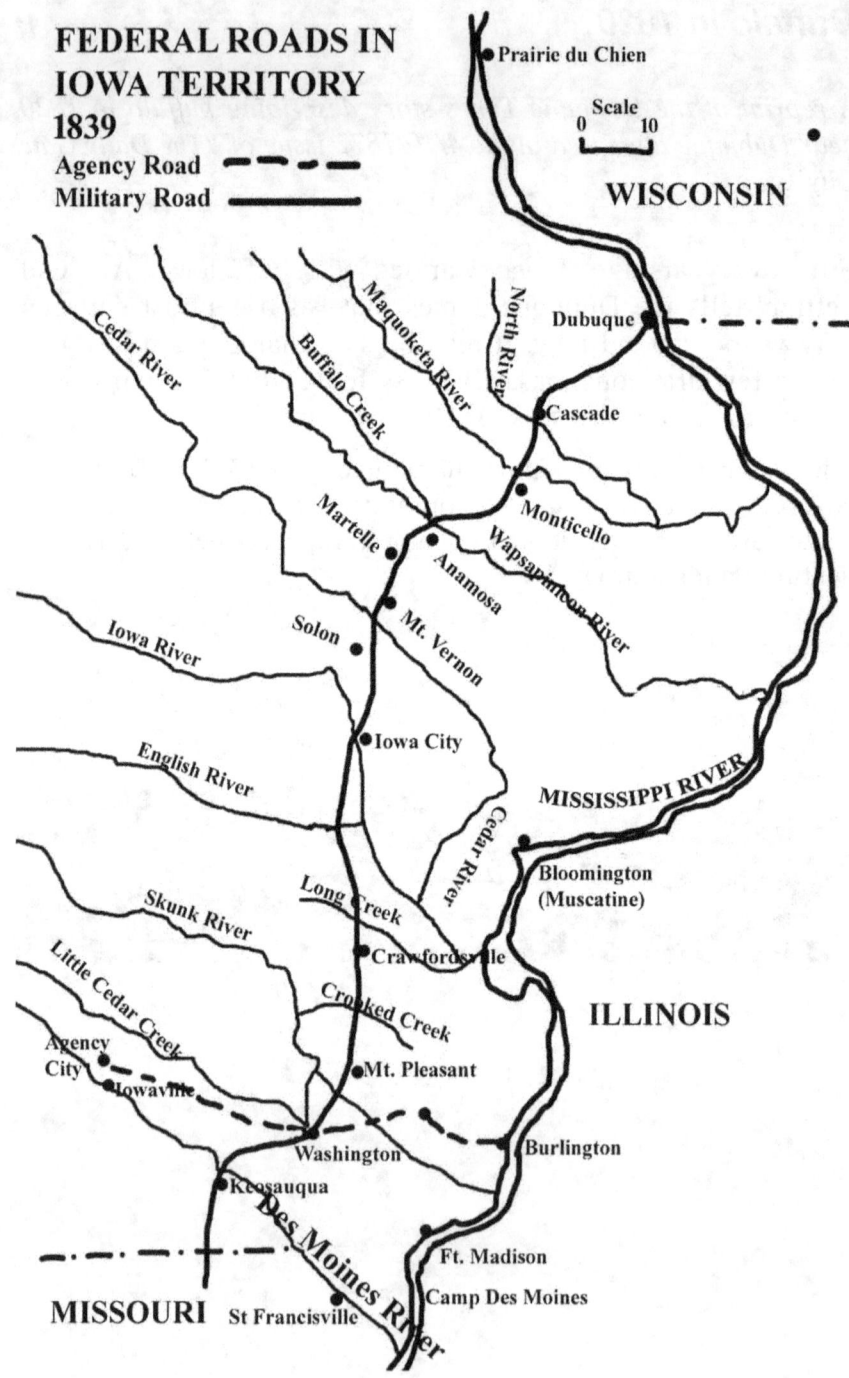

Wedding of Thirty-Five Years Ago
How it was consummated.

A story of how dedicated the pioneer preacher was, travel on the Midwest frontier and a short story of a pioneer wedding appeared in the Apr. 28, 1881 issue of "The Weekly Gate City"

Rev. John Burgess, M. D., of Keokuk, relates the following story of a marriage ceremony consummated under great difficulties thirty-five years ago:

In the fall of 1846, I had the good luck of being sent to the M__[22] mission, my fourth year in the vineyard of my Master. This was also my first charge as senior preacher. The three previous years I was junior, and have ever since rejoiced of having the wisdom of three good men over me. If this were continued over young men, it would be far better for them, and the church. My colleague was one of the best of men, very lively and good humored, and useful. The country over which our mission extended was of large plains, and also dense woods, intersected by several streams, and it also embraced the great and at times terrible Sciota River. For a good part of the season, miles of acres were overspread with water, for when it snowed or rained, it was very difficult to find its way out. Small rains often swelled the little creeks suddenly, and sometimes great rains came down and raised the river immensely. The time I will now allude to, was late in the month of February. Several hard rains had descended, and the whole open lands, and timber also were quite inundated. At this time a great damp snow succeeded the rains, and all nature was mantled with a white coat. On a Friday morning while passing to my week-day appointment, a gentleman came riding along the road quite briskly, and met me. He seemed a little excited and nervous, but bracing up, said: "See here, my good brother, I want you to marry me next Tuesday at 2 o'clock." "Ah!" said I, is that so, Brother W., and where will it be?" "O, I guess about 8 miles off; it's

---

[22] Presume Methodist

to be over at the house of Mr. L., you know the place. She lives near the Sciota River; so you can meet me and others at the cross roads and we will start early so as to make good time." All was arranged, and by the hour of 4, quite early, I mounted my fleet horse and soon met him and two others, all on horseback, equipped for the occasion. Our ride was through a dense forest, the trees not even blazed, and no trail to guide us. Every step on the open ground was mud and slush, and when we touched the edge of the woods, the whole earth was overspread with water from four to twenty inches in depth. Neither of us knew the exact course by line, but had to judge by the moss on the trees and our traveling instinct or reason. No sooner had we come under the trees than we found that every limb and twig was covered with heavy snow, so that our movements brought it down copiously on our bodies and hand, down our necks, wetting us like to a shower, and all over our horses and saddles, until it was very uncomfortable to sit and ride well. But we moved along, each one thinking himself the best guide; we followed each other as whosoever happened to be ahead in the march. We would cry out, "Take the lead now, you, Mr. Groom; take the lead brother. We fear you have gotten us into a pretty muss[23]." So he, boy-like, would hasten his horse, and the sound echoed loudly, "Come along; go ahead; put on the spurs; all right, we'll soon make shore; the glimmering of land is visible." Bro. W. was merry as a cricket and happy as a lark on a hay stack, full of real, good fun, and as we somewhat tantalized him, he took all as any youth would, for you know we were going to a wedding, and that is the time to be glad. We "kinder" lost our way, and as it is said, "went it blind" for a little distance. All small streams were booming full and raging, but we pitched in and crossed in good glee[24]. Shortly we saw the first opening, and who should we see but the familiar face of a friend, a Baptist preacher. So Brother Carr, who was along, cried out halloo!, Brother Higgins, we feel at home now, for we are all about lost, and are mighty glad to

---

[23] In a state of disorder
[24] Great pleasure or satisfaction.

meet you. He was in his shirt sleeves, on a log, chopping like a good fellow. "Well, well, I declare, what does all this mean, and where are you all going," he asked. I replied, O just over here to a wedding! "To a wedding? And who's going to be wedded such a gloomy day as this? O, this young brother, we all said, pointing to Brother W. "Well, well," said Brother H, "I think he has lots of courage and high ambition, and is full of royal hope to undertake the job these times." We all said come Brother H-, come and go with us and show the lost travelers the way. How far is it over to Mr. L's? O, I guess about five miles, but I doubt if we can get through for the water is awful-high, but nothing like trying, and I suppose this is a desperate case." He ran in the cabin like a noble fellow, put on his wammus[25] and hat, bridled his old gray mare, and with a blanket, without any saddle, mounted, and we were off in the purest of spirit. In about two miles ride we came to a bayou where the stream had filled and backed up for at least one half furlong[26] wide, so we feared to enter, but said, now Brother H. You are a good Baptist and never fear water, so lead us, and in he plunged, and

down he dipped, clear over the horse and up to his neck, then turned his horse and swam out. If we had died the next hour, we could not have refrained from laughter, at his misfortunate leap.

---

[25] a warm work jacket made usually in a belted cardigan style and of sturdy knitted or woven fabric.
[26] an eighth of a mile, 220 yards

We all went up about a half mile further, so crying out "take the lead," once more Brother H. as you are a good navigator, and in he went and crossed, holding his feet and legs on the horses' shoulder; but he had mercy on me as the parson, or on the groom so nicely fixed in his wedding garments, and he told us to go up a little higher. We did so and passed over midside to our horses. A short distance more, and we met another like embarrassment,  and to be safe and sure we rode about a furlong up stream and crossed where it only came to our saddle skirts. After a good laugh at our good leader, and also many thanks, we came, directly, in sight of a small clearing of a few acres, and the house within a mile and a half of the river. This was where the expected bride lived. Just at this moment, as we reached the place, no language can describe the scene and effect produced by our arrival. First, the river had so swollen that nearly all the near neighbors had fled to this hut, a one story hewed log cabin; and others not so adjacent had all been driven to the higher land or dry spots, with what little clothing and stock they had; for all their cabins were in and under water, and some had been swept away. This one was on the highest little knoll, supposed to be very safe, and in all recollection, the river had never before this time, come within a half a mile of the house. Now the mad water was rushing past within thirty feet of the door. In this cabin was a large six feet wide fireplace, with a jam about four feet high, and a roaring log heap fire burning. It was a chilly snow and began freezing soon after we came. There were twelve or fifteen refuges there, avoiding the flood, among whom was a

Campbellite[27] preacher, also his family. Our coming was such a surprise to all, but especially to the bride, who had no idea of us, or of the groom being on hand, and supposed it impossible for any one to reach the premises. She was therefore perfectly unprepared. She stood by the firejam[28], with hands and head against it, and wept with disappointment and confusion; for had she had the least thought of our coming, she would have been ready in her bridal attire. But matters must go ahead now, after all this trouble. So I went and touched her on her shoulder and said, "Come how my good sister, cheer up, this will never happen again as long as you live; so take things as they come all right, and make yourself ready, and let the wedding go on." Then for a few minutes while she assuaged[29] her grief, we all talked of the weather and flood, and the preacher said, "Well, for ten days we never had a glimpse of the sun, until this morning, when it broke through a cloud, and O, you don't know how happy we were when we saw that cloud open, and the rays come down on us; we fairly shouted, for I tell you a gloom and almost despair had settled upon us all; we feared and prayed and wept, and did not know what to do." I interrupted him, and said "Why, if you had started, you'd been a Methodist." He replied: "Yes; we felt a little that way; but if the river had risen one foot more, it would, as you see, been in this cabin; but this morning it came to a standstill." As this Christian minister told us all this sad and doleful story, tears filled all our eyes. Then said I: "Now come, gentlemen, let us all go out a while, and the ladies will fix her up and then call us in, and we'll tend to this little affair quickly." Out we went, and hopped and walked about the door, beat our feet up and down, and kept warm as possible for half an hour or so; and the door was opened, and we entered into the marriage ceremonies. I said: "Now, Brother W., please take the lady by her right hand, and stand near the window." Then all of us, about

---

[27] follower of Thomas Campbell – Disciples of Christ claim origin from him
[28] Side post of a fireplace holding mantle
[29] to soothe, calm, or mollify

twenty, besides several children, rose to our feet, and I proposed, that, "Under these peculiar circumstances, we will sing a few verses;" so repeating the hymn:[30]

> **"When I can read my title clear**
> **To mansions in the skies,**
> **I'll bid farewell to every fear**
> **And wipe my weeping eyes,"** etc.

Which was sung as I never heard before, so sweetly, with abounding thanks, after which the ceremony was performed as cheerfully as possible; but somehow the whole scene and surroundings made it a solemn, though pleasant affair. Hearty congratulations were given to the clever couple, though the Baptist preacher proposed to the groom, to which we all willingly agreed, that he return with us to guide us safely back, and in a few days the waters would abate[31], and then he could return; for, said he, this room is now too much crowded. But Brother W. declined promptly, and seemed inclined to tarry with his captured bird. Then we mounted our horses and moved rapidly homeward. Surely we tendered numerous thanks to the excellent "free will Baptist preacher" for guiding us over, and through the deep waters of trouble. Whenever, after that time, he and we met our pleasures increased. As a young man, I felt proud with the "five" in my pocket. Now, as the dear couple are both on the shining shore, I will tell you something: Brother W. was a widower, seventy two years old, and sister L. was a widow fifty-six; well matched lived several years happily in Christian love, and departed to dwell on the banks of the river of life - beyond the flood.

---

[30] https://www.youtube.com/watch?v=_z6qrV_hQ6A
[31] To retreat, subside, or decline

West Point Lot Sales 9/10/1836

A story about the first "land Sales" in the Wisconsin Territory, the Ratlan – Points feud, saved from near starvation by a cold snap, strong whisky as a defense and entertaining fist fights appeared in "The Daily Gate City" on Nov. 4, 1870

The proprietors were all temperance men, and one or two of them elders in the old bluestocking[32] Presbyterian church, and they had set apart a liberal plat of ground to their late minister, and he was coming to settle there, and they had arranged to build a meeting house and organize a church. To be a "hard shell"[33] Baptist was then respectable with the settlers, to be a Campbellite, was passable; and to be a Methodist, could be tolerated; but they felt it was asking rather too much to come among them and propagate temperance and bluestocking Presbyterianism. It was strongly whispered that this was a bad set to settle a new country - in fact, it was whispered pretty loudly. The proprietors were very anxious to have their sale a success. They were all Kentuckians, and at that time had seen but few Yankees; still they had picked up some, Yankee ideas, and as nearly all the settlers were from the south, they concluded to make, on the day of the sale, a regular old-fashioned barbecue. No sooner was this known, than the hard shells themselves softened, and offers from all quarters were made to take charge of the roasting department of the barbecue, and the worst of enemies became the best of friends. Both the sale and barbecue were a grand success, plenty to eat for all, and well cooked, no one intoxicated, everything cheerful and pleasant. The sale amounted to about $2,300.

---

[32] Leading church promoting morality and women's rights. Temperance, anti-prostitution, anti-pornography, etc. Nick-named from un-dyed bluish wool stockings.

[33] "Primitive Baptists" who opposed all Sunday schools, Temperance societies, Bible societies, Missionary societies, etc., and held it to be a great sin to receive money for preaching.

Now, reader, do not say, "That is no sum at all." You must recollect that this was before most of you were born and long before the days of army sutlers[34], commissaries[35], quartermasters, and shoddy contractors during a great war.

There were about two hundred people at the sale; many brought their families. Among others, there were a dozen or so of candidates for the legislature. The territory of Wisconsin had then just been organized, and an election for the legislature ordered. There were then but two counties in the territory, west of the Mississippi - Des Moines and Dubuque - Pine river, between Bloomington (now Muscatine) and Davenport, being the dividing line on the river. Des Moines County was entitled to three members of the Council and six members in the House. The main question at that election was the county line. Almost everybody had a town, and they wanted the new counties made to suit their towns and county seats. All the candidates at this sale were, of course, in favor of making a county that would make West Point the county seat; but I suspect the promise was forgotten, much after the fashion of the present day.

There, was a very great immigration to the territory in that year, and scarcely any grain raised. The result was, short rations; and to add to this, it was an early winter, closing the river with ice, and cutting off supplies from that quarter. The town of Denmark had been located that season by an enterprising company of Yankees, headed by Fox, Epps, and Shed. Taking time in advance, they had gone into Illinois and bought a small drove of hogs to drive on foot, expecting to get back before the river closed; but when they got to the river it was full of ice, so that the ferry could not run, but fortune favored them, by the ice blocking so that they drove over their hogs on the ice the next day. This pork almost literally kept the people from starving until other supplies could be got from Illinois. The winter was long, cold, and dreary, and almost the entire supplies of every kind had to come from Illinois, and had to be hauled more than one hundred miles, and were sold at enormous prices.

---

[34] civilian merchants who sells provisions to an army
[35] a government official charged with oversight

But during that whole long dreary winter, a Methodist preacher by the name of Cartwright, living a few miles west of Burlington, traveled the circuit of what is now Des Moines, Lee, and  Van Buren counties, never missing an appointment. From West Point to Keosauqua there was nothing but a trail, and that covered with snow and ice, and few settlers; yet rain or snow, he was always on time. I fear there are few preachers, Methodist or otherwise, now in that circuit, who would be willing to go through such trials, with the fare and same pay. If alive, I hope this noble man has an easy place now; if dead, he has his reward.

West Point, and immediate vicinity, up to its being cursed with getting the county Seat, for which it struggled so long, was a model town for sobriety and moral character. By nature it is one of the handsomest places in the State; but it has now, by railroads, been thrown into an eddy[36], and has settled down into, a quiet, democratic, Dutch town. When first settled, it was a sort of halfway place of meeting, between a clan that lived on the Skunk, headed by a notorious ruffian by the name of Hamp Raltan, and an almost equally hard set that lived on Sugar Creek, headed by a family by the name of Points. These parties would regularly meet in West Point on Saturdays, run scrub races, drink whisky, and make themselves generally disagreeable to the good citizens. The Raltan crowd were horse thieves and regular desperadoes. They finally became so bad that the citizens encouraged the Points party, and they, one Saturday, drove the Raltan party out of the town and finally out of the country; and as the county settled up, the Points party naturally drifted off. John Points was known as the bully of his section, although not at all quarrelsome.

---

[36] Circular movement of water, causing a whirlpool

At that time there was a man by the name of Allan living near where Charleston is now situated. Allan was from Maine, and prided himself on being a Yankee - an article scarce at that time in that section. Allan had heard of Points as the bully of West Point. Points was a Kentuckian. Allan sent him word that he would meet him to West Point on a certain Saturday; that he was from Maine and that he believed a Maine man could whip any Kentuckian. With the Saturday Allan and Points met the first time. Their friends formed a ring and the two men went to work. Points had ten friends to Allan's one, but no one said a word; perfect fair play was observed, until Allan said he was whipped. It was a rough and tumble fight, and never were two men more evenly matched, and seldom better men. The fight was long and desperate; both men were a mangled mass when through. Old Father Brand, a Virginia gentleman of the old school, who had graduated into a Justice of the Peace, commanded the peace, and commanded the power of the commonwealth to stop the fight; but it was to no purpose, no one obeyed, and the commonwealth stood still until the fight was all over, when he had them both arrested. Each one pleaded that the fight was merely in fun; no harm whatever was intended; that it was merely to test the fighting qualities of Maine and Kentucky. Allan was very eloquent, that Points, at least, should not be fined as he was the victor; but the Justice could not be convinced that it was legal for men to fight in fun. He fined them five dollars each, but I never heard of the fine being collected.

The ambition in West Point, in the early day of its greatness, was to be the county seat, and after many trials and many failures, it finally succeeded in getting the court house. Up to that time Solomon had had a monopoly of selling whisky for the thirsty and the traveling man; but during court, John Kenneday, of Fort Madison, opened out a caboose[37], where he was supposed to sell "choice" red eye. Near the town lived a noble old man by the name of Creel, an old-fashioned Kentuckian, who kept up the Kentucky rule of taking a dram when he went to town, and meeting a friend, they went to Kenneday's and took a couple of

---

[37] a kitchen on the deck of a ship; galley, slang for a cheap saloon and restaurant.

drinks. Creel then went into the court house, and not liking something that was said or done, very emphatically objected. Judge Mason was on the bench at the time, and he fined Creel $5.00. The next morning the old man went to Mason's boarding house and told the judge that he did not object to or complain of the fine, but that he really thought the fine should have been put on Kenneday and not him. The judge, in his kind way asked, "Why so?" "Why," says the, old man, "I go to town generally about once a week, or once in two weeks, and according to my old custom, I go to Solomon's and I take two drinks, I treating some one and he treating me. We are used to Solomon's whisky; it is not strong, and does not hurt us, we understand it; but here comes this man Kenneday, from Fort Madison, with his new kind of whisky, that we know nothing about, and I take only my two drinks, and it intoxicates me so that I am fined; now, it was not me, but Kenneday, that was to blame." The judge at once agreed to, and did, remit the fine.

Another fighting scene of that day was laughable in the extreme. Among the early settlers in West Point was a family of Dodds, the old man a little nob[38] of a man that did not weigh more than one hundred and twenty five pounds, but who had been a celebrated fighter, in Tennessee, in his day, and two sons, Orrin and Warren, both now good citizens of Arkansas. Orrin had a store on the southeast corner of the town; the doggery[39] was on the northeast corner. There was a little path from the grocery up to Dodd's store, beat through the grass. One beautiful evening, just about sunset, a big, blustering man by the name of Driscoll from Kentucky, was boasting at the grocery of how many men he had whipped, and declaring, with boisterous oaths, that he could whip any man of his age. Dodd was by, but he had lost his voice, so that he could only whisper; but he goes up to Driscoll, who was twice as large as he was, and asked him how old he was. Driscoll said he was sixty-five. Dodd, without saying a word started slowly up the path to his son's store, who was at the time, sitting out by the door. When he got there he whispered; "Orrin, old Driscoll says that he can whip

---

[38] A person of wealth or high position
[39] a cheap Saloon

any man of his age. He is sixty-five; I am seventy-two. Will I whip him? Orrin answered, "If you can make anything by it." The old man, without saying another word, turned, and deliberately walked back the same path to the grocery, and goes up to Driscoll and says: "You say you can whip any man of your age. You are sixty-five; I am seventy-two;" and 'diff he took him, knocking him down, when he jumped on him. Driscoll commenced hallooing "murder! murder!!" The bystanders took off Dodd, when he again slowly and quietly marched up the same path to his son's store, and said, "I whipped him," and that was the last of it. Driscoll was badly hurt, and never got drunk in town after that. It made him a good citizen.

The article of my friend Toole, and your article giving Gov. Lucas credit for his efforts in favor of public schools, made me recollect an incident of the first Iowa Legislature. Toole was a member from Louisa County and I from Lee, and we both wanted to get some territory from Des Moines County. Toole wanted three miles from the north tier of townships of the county, and I wanted to get the fractional township across Skunk River, embracing Denmark. We had both introduced bills for that purpose, and we then went one evening to see the Governor, to urge him not to veto the bills if we could pass them. Toole in his oily manner introduced the subject of his wants. The Governor, at once, with his hair stiffer than I thought I had ever seen it, said: "No, sir; I will not sign any bill that divides townships." Then, pointing to my bill, which had just come in and been put on his book, "There is a bill I will veto if it passes. Township organizations and public schools are the life and protection of free people. Of all things, public schools are the most important to the people and they can only be properly organized by townships. No, sir, I will allow no township to be divided:

No man ever exerted himself more for public schools, temperance, and Christianity than did Lucas during his administration as Governor. All honor to him for his noble stand at that time.

A Typical Iowa Cabin & Free Mail Delivery

A description of life in the 1830's and the uses of a new cabin was given in "The Gate City" on Jan. 23, 1898

Birmingham Enterprise: Now we will get back among the old settlers again. In 1837-8 we had to go to Van Buren (now Keosauqua) for our mail and pay 25 cents for each letter received. After a time we had our mail sent to Philadelphia - now Kilbourne. It was a flourishing young town, doing business in the stores, blacksmith shop, tannery, etc. It had a good country trade. After Birmingham sprung up we got a post office of our own. Our first postmaster, Jacob Lawton, was a native Yankee - a young man, tall and slender, quite talkative. I will give the young people a description of our first post office building and how Mr. Lawton lived when he got married. The post office building was a log building about 16x20 feet, one room. Now take notice of how one large room can be utilized to the best advantage. First the post office was kept in it, then his wife and stove. It was bedroom, parlor, kitchen and dining room. Mr. Lawton was a wheelwright by trade and made chairs. He had his turning-lathe in the room, made big spinning-wheels to spin wool, little wheels to spin flax, and chairs to sell. And he was a gunsmith and repaired guns. Not only all this, but they lived in that room until they had four children. After a time Mrs. Lawton died there. Some of the children were quite small when their mother died, but the father kept the children - three daughters and one son - together for several years. Some days they had nothing to eat but mush and milk. The old gentleman was over 80 years old and living with his son at last report. Before Mr. Lawton married he would put his letters in his hat when, he had business away. When he met any one that had a letter in the office he would take off his hat and deliver their letters, but there were not so many letters then as now. So you see we had free mail delivery long before the large cities. James Steel, a one-armed man, was postmaster after Lawton. It was a few years later when the last purchase of the territory was settling up. When Mr. Steel was postmaster we had a four-horse coach line from Keokuk to Des Moines. One left each end of the route every morning. The driver carried a big horn, which he would blow while approaching the post office.

There was a town laid off in those early days every few miles along the Des Moines River in Van Buren County.

The Meek family settled in Bonaparte about 1837. They established the first water mill on the Des Moines River. It was a saw and grist mill. The Meek brothers worked together in the mill business for many years. Their grist mill ran night and day for several years, and they made a success of the business. People went a distance of considerably more than fifty miles. Many people came from, Missouri to their mill. Money was very scarce in those early days and we would take several days provisions with us, so we could stay until our grinding was done. There being no place to stay in the mill, we would arrange great log heaps in the winter to burn at night, while we slept outdoors. We slept, cooked and ate around those burning log heaps in all kinds of weather.

Quite a number of towns along the river died. I remember the names of several of them - Lexington, Columbus, Iowaville, Black Hawk and Rochester. Rochester was on the river east of the poor farm. It was quite a thrifty place and tried to get the county seat, but Keosauqua came out ahead and then Rochester died a natural death and there is no land mark to tell where she lived.

The first justice of the peace in this vicinity was a Mr. Jackson. He lived in a cabin in Lick Creek, near Philadelphia. There was a couple went to him to be married. It was, his first marriage ceremony, and he wound up as follows: He told the groom to salute, the bride. The young man did not understand the meaning of the word salute, until the squire explained it to him to kiss her. That ended the ceremony.

Incidents of the Early Days in Keokuk

A freshet[40] scare and beastly investment in Keokuk are described in "The Constitution Democrat" on May 18, 1892.

During this rainy season is a pertinent occasion to reproduce a story told by the late Col. J. M. Reid, as it begins with a description of a freshet which came near causing an old settler's death.

"An old settler butcher came from Baltimore. Md., set up a shop with knife and cleaver, and located his slaughter house at the lower end of Bloody Run, sometimes called Maiden Run, and again Jiggery's Branch, near the river's bluff. Just beyond it is low ground, and not much further on, the river into which it empties. The butcher always went down to the slaughter house at daylight.

One night there came a tremendous rain storm. Next morning Bloody Run had overflowed its banks, and the heretofore sluggish stream was running in torrents. The butcher started to the slaughter house, driving his favorite old gray horse "Gramalkin," and in trying to cross the stream; horse wagon and driver were carried down with the flood.

He said his prayers, expecting instant death, but in passing on the friendly branches of an overhanging elm tree were seen and seized by him and he was saved. The horse and wagon were carried onward by the mad waters of the resistless tide, and the wagon was found weeks afterward four miles below at Alexandria, Mo. But; the faithful Gramalkin, now food for catfish, was never seen or heard of more. Like a faithful soldier he died with, the harness on. He could have no funeral procession, no tomb in enduring granite to perpetuate his memory, and his master growing pathetic, instead of an

---

[40] spring thaw of river or stream when breaking ice can block the stream and cause deadly flooding along the stream or river.

epitaph wrote a poem which rhymed very much like those sweet and euphonious[41] words Frederick and May-Pole.

The butcher then rushed into speculation - bought two cub bears, was offered fifty dollars for them at home, but took them to St. Louis to market. He marched up street holding the chain fastened to the collar of each pet in either hand, feeling good and stepping higher than a blind horse.

A crowd followed him; he was offered $100 for the bears. But, no! That was not enough- he had set his heart oh a higher figure. The boys, now resolved on sport, got sharp sticks, and prodding the bears in the ribs they grew frantic. When he ran at one who tormented one bear some one on the outskirts prodded the other. But he held on to the chains while he was alternately jerked by the infuriated beasts, first on one side and then on the other while he pleaded and protested to no purpose. The boys were hard-hearted and resolved to have a free menagerie of their own, and they had it. The owner of the bears got sick, exhausted and disgusted; there was no rest for the wicked. A stranger now came along and benevolently offered him five dollars for the two bears, and John Hinder,

---

[41] pleasing to the ear.

of the "People's Market," sold out his show and came home with his eye-teeth cut, resolved to stick to hogs and horned cattle and let wild beasts alone.

A French milliner brought on the crisis and hurried up the sale, coming out at her door just as one of the cubs was about to charge on her show window."

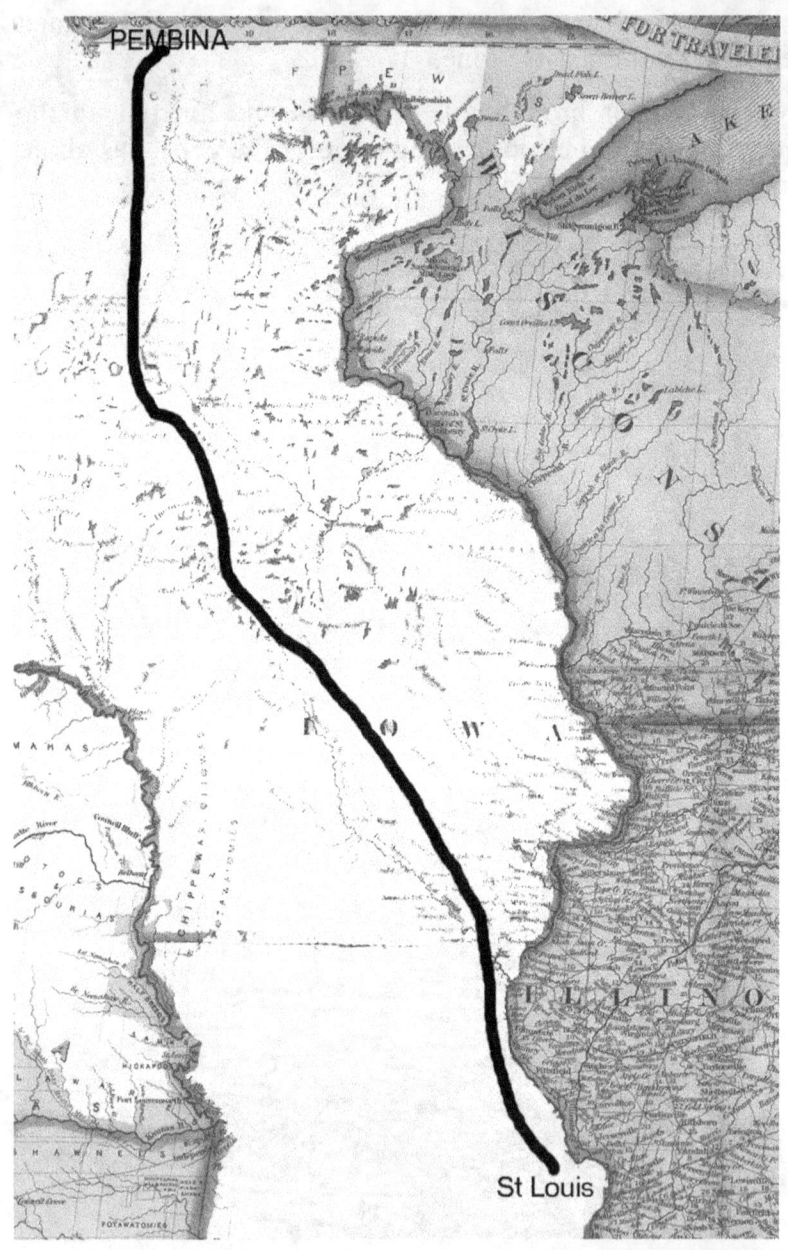

Approximate 1000 mile route of the 1815 cattle drive from St Louis to Lord Selkirk's Hudson Bay Settlement on the Red River, now Pembina, ND

1815 Cattle drive from St. Louis, MO to Canada

Consider this: Just 9 years after Lewis and Clark returned home(1815), Lord Selkirk, who resided in Scotland, ordered cattle from someone in New York, who sub-contracted with residents of St. Louis, MO to drive cattle to the Red River settlement of the Hudson Bay Company (Pembina, ND today). There were no roads, no bridges, no maps, nor anyone who could know the way. It was almost totally through Indian Territory. The only thing they had was an accurate latitude and longitude, similar to what sailors used, and that the settlement was on the Red River way up north. The shortest route today is 1000 miles by road. They were on foot or horseback, no wagon would make it, and all but one made it home safely! In the spring of 1816, the Northwest Fur Company orchestrated the massacre of settlement, killing the governor and 30 others and imprisoning the rest, which explains why Pembina has no record of the drive. As it turns out, in 1820, Pembina was declared USA territory instead of British Canadian by virtue of the 1818 treaty of Ghent with Canada.

In comparison, The famous Texas cattle drives to Abilene, KS were after 1860 and covered about 700 miles over the established Chisholm Trail. Story is in "The Gate City" on Oct. 19, 1870 and is written by A.W. Harlan as told to him by Giles Sullivan..

"The principal event of our story occurred in 1815, just at the close of the last British war; but even previous to that date, Lord Selkirk, a Scottish nobleman, had planted his colony on the Red River of the North. The latitude and longitude had been taken intolerably accurate. Now, if the reader wishes to thoroughly understand the situation, he can take a map and look along the northern border of Minnesota, look up Pembina, ND (a locality just now somewhat interesting.) take a careful survey of the locality, note the rivers and lakes intervening between and that point and the mouth of the Missouri River, and he may begin to comprehend the situation.

Lord Selkirk's colonists, as yet, had not cattle; he made a contract with some citizens of New York (as well as I can remember, for several circumstances and names have been by me forgotten) to deliver to his agent at his colony, five hundred head of cattle. A check or bill of exchanges, drawn by Lord Selkirk himself made payable to the original contractor, was to be delivered by the agent on the delivery of the cattle. Around St. Charles, Missouri, was the nearest point at which cattle could be procured. The original contractor came to Missouri and himself contracted with old Doc Carr and big Lewis Musick to deliver to Selkirk's agent so many hundred head of milch[42] cows and a certain number of bulls. So far all was correct.

Carr and Musick were energetic men; had some money of their own, paid a part down for cattle – the sellers trusting them for the balance until they should receive their pay for the cattle.

The winter had been mild, spring opened early, and they had made a start up the Mississippi bottoms in February. Giles Sullivan hired to assist them as far as the Des Moines – he was then a young man. The whole drove crossed the Des Moines just about[43] where the ferry is now kept, the first day of March 1815, and the feed was tolerably plenty – a fact unknown since that time. Those cattle were grazed on that beautiful scope of prairie where Vincennes – a station on the D.V. Railroad – is now situated. Sullivan here left them. He and one other man then wended their way about one hundred and twenty miles, to the settlements near St. Charles.

After resting some few days, they took up their line of march up the divide thro' String Prairie, towards Big Mound. The first time I ever crossed that prairie, when near where Absalom Anderson now lives, Sullivan said that Carr and Musick must have passed about the same place with a large drove of cattle more than nineteen years before, but no trace was left, nor was there any sign of human beings, save ourselves.

The drove kept on the prairie, between the dividing waters of the Skunk and the Des Moines rivers, and I may as well here observe

---

[42] Middle English word for milk giving, also German in origin.
[43] In the near vicinity of

that at that time the Iowa Indians held possession of this section of country. It was not until 1818 that the Sac and Fox Indians fought, whipped and drove them from their village, where Iowaville now stands.

The drove moved on, keeping on the divide without any serious difficulty, until they reached the country of the Chippewa's. Here straggling members of that tribe began to hang around, and follow them from day to day. The Indians were mounted on small ponies. Lewis Musick told his men to ride over on every convent opportunity, himself setting the example. The Chippewa's kept on increasing in numbers daily, until one day more than a hundred painted warriors were seen approaching. The Indians evidently expected a small fight. Musick told his men to keep driving the cattle ahead; to pay no attention to the Indians; to ride right over them if they got in their way. Big Lewis Musick was almost a giant, of herculean force, and rode a remarkably large horse; and made it his business to ride over the most conspicuous braves, occasionally taking one of them by the shoulder and hauling him from his pony.

This tribe was at that time at peace with the United States, and did not wish to shed the first blood. They however managed to stampede a few cattle and slaughter them. This delayed the Indians that afternoon.

The drovers kept on all that night, and by the next day were in the country of the Sioux, where the Chippewa's did not dare to follow.

In this latitude the large white wolves began to appear in considerable numbers.

They were something new to the Missourian drovers. They seemed to follow on from day to day, just out of idle curiosity, and did not seem disposed to attack either men or cattle, and when the drove would halt at night or noon, the wolves would get on some conspicuous place, form in line, set on their haunches, and view the strange cavalcade.

At last, to the great joy of both drovers and colonists, the settlement was reached. The drovers had finished their arduous task. The agent was well pleased with the cattle. Then the colonists had milk for the first time in several years. The cattle were counted and the check delivered. So far all right.

The next thing for the drovers was to go home. They started and followed the trail of the cattle into what is now the southern portion of Minnesota; and here in a vast expanse of prairie some of the men differed about the course to be pursued. Most of the men followed Carr and Musick, who had a compass to direct them, and all of them reached the Mississippi at some point below St. Paul, and most of them came home in Indian canoes. The two men that left the main party and took a course more to the right, struck the head waters of the Des Moines and followed down that stream, thus being compelled[44] to cross all the tributaries. The weather becoming wet, the streams were all swollen. The men had to swim, and in swimming one stream, probably above Des Moines, one of those men got his rifle tangled in some vines, and in trying to save his gun, got tangled himself and was drowned or at least the survivor so reported to the settlement. I have frequently heard their names, but have forgotten both of them long ago.

The next thing for Carr and Musick was to get their check or exchange cashed. Sullivan could not give all the names of the men connected in this transaction; consequently this portion of the narrative must be incomplete. But, as Carr and Musick were only sub-contractors, the check had to pass through the hands of the original contractor, and by some "Hocus Pocus" Old Dick Carr and Big Lewis Musick were cheated out of every dollar of their hard earned money. The result was that they could not pay all the balance on the cattle that they had bought of those early settlers about St. Charles, Missouri. But the grievous loss must be borne, and was, borne by some cheerfully, by others despondently. All survived the loss, except Lewis Musick.

Big Lewis Musick was an enterprising, proud spirited man. He paid as far as he could, and that was all he could do. He could not bear to look a man in the face to whom he honestly owed money. He became despondent, seemed to sink under his misfortunes and soon died. Thus ended the career of one of nature's noblemen. He

---

[44] force or oblige (someone) to do something

died bankrupt, not for the want of energy or honesty, but because one villainous Yankee cheated him, for all reports that I ever heard concurred in saying that Lord Selkirk and his agent both acted honorably throughout the whole transactions.

As for Old Dick Carr, he did not despair. He had some friends in St. Louis that offered to furnish the goods and teams for the first expedition that ever went from Missouri to Santa Fe. This was several years before Thomas H. Benton got an appropriation from Congress to make a road to that place.

That expedition made their own road across the plains and over mountains, and were eminently successful. The profits were amicably divided, and Old Dick Carr was enabled to pay all his debts and have a competence left. He spent a few years of his old age quietly, and then he, too, took the journey to that bourne from whence no traveler returns."

Overland in 1870

An account of travel through Iowa in 1870 and how much it has changed over the years. The same trip today takes just a few minutes on super highways and less than 1% of the native prairie is left. Visit a reconstructed prairie at Neal Smith National Wildlife Refuge near Prairie City, Iowa to get an idea of what it was like. Published in "The Daily Gate City" on Jul. 1, 1870

Dear Gate: Four wheels and a pair of horses do not devour distance like the locomotive coach, but if you can only persuade yourself to be in no hurry, how pleasantly they bear you over the verdure[45] of Iowa.

From Keokuk to Des Moines, it is corn and only corn, on the right and on the left, before you and behind you. Only now and then a field of wheat is thrown in by way of reminder that the article will grow on Iowa soil. Everybody tells you that there is a large breadth of corn planted, but only he who goes slowly and observingly over the ground, as we have done, can properly bring his mind to contemplate the millions on millions of this staple likely to be produced by our State this year.

I think it was in 1860, I went from Eddyville to Des Moines by coach. Then there lay along our course thousands of acres of unsubdued, unfenced prairie. This has all passed away. But four unfenced tracts of prairie low lie out in common[46] along the

---

[45] green growth health and vigor
[46] (There are only four unfenced tracts of prairie left along the route)

while line, and one of these has the posts set for the forthcoming fence.

This is very interesting and even wonderful, to the man who cares for the growth of our young State. To the traveler, "by land" they have made it lugubrious[47]. A straight road from Keokuk to Des Moines would consequently cut the sections of land diagonally. To this the farmers say, "No; we can't afford the fencing, and we don't like to have our farms in triangles." The consequence is you go northwest, like a ship tacking at sea, only you can make right angles instead of obtuse angles, and thereby travel half way around all the farms in your route. This is almost literally true from Charleston to Des Moines.

But you remember that you are not in a hurry, that if so, you would have gone by rail. And even if you find you have gone north too far, and have arrived at Fairfield when you thought yourself about to arrive at Libertyville, you do not complain, for you know it was done soberly. It has only a little extended the length and pleasure of the trip.

Des Moines at last. Two days in our pleasant and growing Capital. That government official (nameless here) who not

---

[47] looking or sounding sad and dismal

only loves our "prunes and senna[48]," but who is really and constitutionally a judge of good living, has already eulogized the house kept by Mrs. Shankland, (formerly Mrs. Washburn,) at Des Moines. He said not a word too much in praise of the delightful hospitality which the boarder or traveler may there find. No abomination in Iowa has been so generally and heartily "cussed," as Des Moines hotels. It is a good thing to know that there is one house of entertainment in the place which the traveler leaves with regret.

We find ourselves in Dallas County next, beautiful with its undulating prairies. Not a developed county yet, but rapidly filling up, and with as beautiful fields, wherever tilled, as lie under the sun. Then we strike Guthrie County, and traverse its southern half, coming out near the southwest corner. Once fairly in that county, the scene changes. The sea of prairie which had been before merely undulatory[49], at once becomes tempest tossed and semi-mountainous. The ridges swell to ranges, and the valleys like hidden and winding among the hills. The views are superb, each acclivity[50] unfolding a new scene in a panorama which could scarcely be more picturesque in a country all prairie.

As we go on the houses disappear. We find ourselves in a solitude bounded by the horizon. Scarce a living thing meets the eye. Even the quails, abundant heretofore, have remained behind with civilization.

We travel ten miles without a house. Then a little group of neighbors. Then twelve miles of solitude again. But a solitude full of beauty and bloom. We have seen the like nowhere else. Lilies of the purest carmine[51] abound profusely. The wild verbena was almost as abundant, but with none of the varieties of color found in the cultivated flower. The dwarf red and white wild rose is present everywhere. Besides these there is something which

---

[48] Wild Senna is a native plant with strong laxative properties.
[49] Rolling waves or a smooth, wavelike motion
[50] An upward slope
[51] A deep-red pigment from the cochineal scale

resembles the aster, and a pendulous, trumpet-shaped white flower which I cannot name. The wild oat exists in occasional patches, and wherever found has taken possession, almost excluding the grass.

Rough and wild as this tract of country is, the soil is anything but poor. Fertile fields might be made even on the summit of the ridges, but the absence of timber and want of any other fuel has kept the settlers away. The railroad which runs not many miles distant could supply material for fencing and building. The fuel question is more difficult unless the sloughs[52] shall be found to contain peat.

As we emerge from Guthrie and enter Cass County, the land improves at once, and we find ourselves among beautiful farms again. The Chicago and Rock Island railroad is developing the prairies here very rapidly. Land which two year ago was valued at from fifteen to twenty-five dollars is now held at from twenty-five to fifty. Atlantic, the new county seat, is a railroad town which has suddenly sprung into life and already numbers a thousand or fifteen hundred souls, possibly more. Lewis, the old county seat, seems to have been finished several years ago.

Just west of Lewis we strike the line of Pottawattamie county. We begin to ascend hill after hill, until we reach a table land or pampas[53], of an apparent higher altitude than any we have yet reached. Here is utter solitude again, and we travel for miles and miles without sight of a single living object. Then a settlement gathered around a few hundred acres of timber; then the desolate prairie again for twelve or fifteen miles. A prairie just as fertile as the best, but desolate from want of timber. And so we reach Council Bluffs and Omaha.

I don't care to tell you of these towns. They have been written about ad nauseam[54]. I have thought our gipsey[55] life

---

[52] stagnant wetland, swamp, or shallow lake
[53] plain - fertile lowlands
[54] disgust that has continued so long - to the point of nausea
[55] nomadic or free-spirited

might interest a few. How gipseyish it has been, I have not yet told. Since we left Des Moines each day has had its picnic. As noon arrives, we stop under some shade, if convenient; if not, we draw the carriage up on the open prairie.

One end of a shawl, some six yards long, is fastened to the top iron of the carriage; the bottom fastened with tent pins to the ground. The neck yoke makes an admirable ridge pole, supported by a rough limb of cottonwood.

Other shawls and cushions galore complete the outfit. A spirit lamp, accompanied by a cartload of fuel, in the shape of a bottle of alcohol, makes the tea. A capacious[56] tin lunch-box keeps the bread moist and provisions sweet. A light gun strapped to the buggy top supplies quail, snipe, curlew and field larks, which are cooked at the stopping places over night.

And so we spend the hours, from twelve to four of each day, under the shade of our improvised tent, varying the monotony with reading or napping, as suits the humor of each, and here, under the shade of the self-same-tent, with my letter already too long, I write my good-by.

R.H.G.

---

[56] having a lot of space inside; roomy.

Keokuk Under the Hill

A description of Keokuk in its first days, finding the town of Utica and the power of advertising published in "The Gate City" on Apr. 9, 1899

It was a very small country home on Indian Creek in Van Buren County but it was progress. The first one, before this, was of round logs just as they fell under the axe in the woods, chosen small because there were not many arms or shoulders to lift them in that way of neighborly help that then prevailed, and when put in place that house was quite open between the logs. That was the best that could be done then but this second pioneer home was better. When it came there were more neighbors, more arms and shoulders to lift the fallen burden of the forest, and what counted for much in the matter there were more turkeys and chickens to go on the table that fairly swayed in those days under the load of the hospitalities of pioneer house-raising. So larger trees had been cut down and they were hewn and squared and there was a man in the neighborhood who could build quite a comfortable and draughty chimney. The same artist knew all about chinking and daubing and my father in the supreme comfort of civilization sat in the early afternoon and looked over six volumes of Adam Clarke's commentaries on the Holy Scriptures newly brought up on a flat boat from St. Louis and overland in a broad-tired wagon from what was afterwards known as Alexandria but then as Wood's Mill. And the chinking and daubing artist went on whistling about his work. He had his pleasure in it because it called for somewhat of the same skill that built the pyramids and the Parthenon and St. Paul's. He had to fit together between the logs the pieces of wood that would leave the least possible hole and then with a big trowel reminiscent of mortar throw clay brought up from the nearest creek into the holes and try to cement them into some firmness of purpose that would stand out against an Iowa winter. It was early in the season. The Indian summer was outdoors. The chinker[57] and dauber whistled at his work. And my father intent at his work on Clarke's newly arrived Commentaries was working out some new ideas that next Sunday over at the Lebanon Methodist Chapel would bring Malachi Vinson and Daniel Hitt and Uncle John Spencer to their knees responding and shouting like another Pentecost in great shape. Meantime Sister Mary - "Sis" we all called her - was dividing her time, watching the corn pone in the skillet and the frying of three young squirrels that George, the nimrod[58] of the household, had brought up from the woods that were not a hundred yards away. It would have troubled Brothers Vinson and Hitt and Spencer the next Sunday if they had known just how often my father during the thinking out of that ecstatic sermon had said anxiously to my sister: "Honey, is supper nearly ready?" We called every meal supper then that women's desire to feed men put out anywhere from three hours before sundown up to 4 o'clock the next morning. A woman has two breasts on her bosom and she thinks she has to nourish all mankind of both sexes. You never saw a woman, not the oldest old maid that ever was that didn't begin to squirm and fidget anxiously if she heard any creature say he was hungry. God bless all women! It is in every one of them. The man may be worthless but the woman in the nobility and supreme mission of her sex never gives up the food problem. When those she loves are at stake she would clamor[59] before God her right of way to the tree of life. And I think God would forgive and love her because He sent His Son to the world by way of the gentle village motherhood of the sacred Mary.

---

[57] Someone who fills in cracks between logs with mud and moss or some other material on cabins, etc
[58] a descendant of Ham noted in Genesis as a mighty hunter.
[59] Loud confused shouting

Just before we sat down to that corn pone and squirrel dinner the two oldest boys came back with the word that J.B. Howell and the Des Moines Valley Whig were to go to Keokuk: that the Valley Whig would no longer be a Keosauqua paper but a Keokuk paper. The lard oil lamp sputtered in its frame and made shadows on the hewed log wall. My father tore the well fried flesh off the young squirrels and laid the bones at the side of the plate. There was a feeling of repression and expansion. One could go back and forth comfortably to Keosauqua and get the Valley Whig in an afternoon and stop for an hour at Goddard's and joke with the three girls. But  now the Valley Whig had been taken farther away and was henceforth to be published at Keokuk under the hill. Our news and politics would take on increased importance because of the lengthened radius of their diffusion. As we were on the west side of the Des Moines river our natural road to Keokuk would have been down the west or Missouri "divide" if it had not been for crossing Fox River and the constant uncertainty whether or not it would let you do it. It was not big enough for one of the old-fashioned rope ferries or else was altogether too big for it. Maybe it was because of the character of some of the people that had settled near it but Fox River had no moral character whatever and no qualities of good judgment that you could rely upon for a minute. It was either shrunk up into little patches of green water and black earth with ugly black mud turtles sprawling on logs that had given up the battle of life, or it was foaming and roaring all over the country a mile beyond its proper banks. It is an absurd stream or was then. No man could put a ferry into a river that either had no water at all or would make the ferryman swim a mile across country to get to his boat.

So we went to Ely's Ford or Keosauqua and crossed the Des Moines River and went to Keokuk the south "divide," passing 'Squire Nixon's and "Utica." There was no trouble about finding Nixon's; it was always there but no one was ever able to find Utica. It was one of the despairs of several years of my life. A town was an event in early Iowa. One couldn't afford to miss one. When you got fairly beyond, West Point you began to look out for Utica. It was a few miles ahead. The afternoon would pass and all at once you would find yourself at "Captain Miller's" on the Keosauqua Hill Road and you would cry with a sharp little gasp of amazed inquiry: "Where's Utica?" "Oh, we passed it some time ago." The matter doesn't interest me so much now because I am an old man but maybe ever one owes it to himself and his fellows to strip life of illusions. If so it may be my bounden duty to find Utica before I die.

The Valley Whig began to come from Keokuk instead of Keosauqua. The odd thing about it all is that I do not remember anything whatever that was in the paper about the politics or great events of the time but I remember the advertisements, the allusions to business and professional men and this or that local incident as if photographed for me. It was years afterwards that I went to Keokuk but I knew it as well as its oldest inhabitants. I knew "Smith Hamill, "Cleghorn & Harrison," "A.L. Connable," "Hugh W. Sample," "L.B. Fleak," "C. Garber," "D.A. Humphrey," and scores of others as if I had made them. I, the country boy who had never seen "Keokuk under the hill," could have given pointers in knowledge of its localities even to its own busy business men. That was not before the unhappy days of Friday "compositions" in the schools and the traps they set for forlorn and badly tempted souls in whom the normal desire for salvation is probably what it should be. One Friday an older boy who had got to that self-conscious stage that he took pains with his hair and looked at the girls without dropping his eyes read a "composition" about the long lines of ox-teams, the wagons piled high with store boxes, the bent white cover ready for the storm, the drivers joking with each other as they drove out Main street upon the country roads and towards the village and country store, and cracked their whips upon the flanks of the straining oxen. A boy is cruel as death but seldom mean. I said nothing before the teacher or the girls but when I got him to himself I sputtered at him with angry defiance: "You stole that from the Valley Whig: you know you did." It was a picture of Keokuk under the hill in the old days.

Early Iowa Indians

A.L. Cruze *tells of AW Harlan's description of Black Hawk and what he considered his greatest gift to the conquered Ioway Indian Nation is printed in the Mar. 17, 1898 issue of "The Gate City."*

A. W. Harlan, a grand and good old man, who resides near - the little town of Croton, in Lee County, Iowa, is an old pioneer who came to Iowa in 1834. Mr. Harlan, in early days, became acquainted and became somewhat confidential with some of the chiefs of the Fox and Sacs. He at one time visited the battlefield, in Van Buren County, where Black Hawk defeated the Iowans in a hard fought battle. Mr. Harlan visited this battle ground in company with Pashepaho, who was one of Black Hawk's aids. Mr. Harlan says of Pashepaho that he was a man of great judgment and courage, a man whose worth and not his ancestry won him a high place in the councils of his tribe. The cause of the war between the Fox and Sacs and Ioways was caused by the Iowa Indians insulting a few of the Sac and Fox Indian women, who were camped on the Mississippi river, near Montrose, while their husbands were away from the camp at the above named place hunting.

This insult of the Sac and Fox women by the Iowa Indians caused the Indians to break their camp and hasten[60] back to their village on Rock River, in Illinois, to gather together men to avenge the insult they had received. It is said that Black Hawk had much difficulty in restraining his braves from going on the war path at that time of the year. He prevailed in having his braves wait until the next summer before marching into the country of the Ioway's. With the coming of summer Black Hawk made due preparation for an invasion into the territory of the enemy. All things being ready, the invading warriors marched from their village to the Mississippi river. After reaching the river they floated down the river at night, and camped on the islands during the day to keep themselves secreted from their enemies' scouts, who were out on the front to watch for the coming of the Sac and Fox, whom they were expecting to come out against them.

---

[60] To speed up

Part of Black Hawk's force divided at some point on the Mississippi and marched overland through Illinois and crossed the Mississippi river at or near Fort Edward, now Warsaw, Ill, and expected to march on the camp of the Ioway's and attack it on side, while Black Hawk's force was to continue down the Mississippi river to Montrose and march overland and arrive at the camp of the Ioway's at the same time that Pashepaho's force. The plan of attack was for Pashepaho to open the battle on one side of the village; then Black Hawk would attack the enemy on the opposite side. This plan was mis-carried by Pashepaho's arriving at the village about one-half day before Black Hawk's force. Pashepaho then commenced the attack, but we are told he fought for awhile and then retreated to join forces with Black Hawk. This premature attack of Pashepaho before Black Hawk was in striking distance angered Black Hawk so much so, that he and Pashepaho had quite a lively exchange of uncomplimentary words with each other. Here Black Hawk moved on the Ioways and after a hard, fought battle he succeeded in completely breaking their power as a nation. After the battle was over, Black Hawk, we are told, offered to receive any of the Ioways who would accept of it, as members of his tribe, with all the rights and privileges of that tribe. Some of the Ioway's Indians accepted the offer and some did not. This offer of Black Hawk's, in offering to receive his late enemies as brothers into his tribe; Black Hawk considered the noblest act of his life. So much so, that he wished to be buried on the spot of ground where he had so generously offered the olive branch of peace to his fallen, for Mr. Harlan is probably the only living white man who was shown over the battlefield by those who had participated in the fight. Mr. Harlan says of Black Hawk that he was a true Indian. His first thought was always for his people. That he accepted the inevitable because he was powerless to stand against the encroachments of the whites. Mr. Harlan, in common with all the early settlers, speaks well of Black Hawk, and all men who knew, him regarded Black Hawk as a man of his word.

Origin of the name Devil Creek

This personal account of how the Indians named Devil Creek was given by A. W. Harlan in the Oct 1, 1870 issue of "The Gate City".

About the 1st of November, in the fall of 1834, while I was haying with Giles Sullivan, below Camp Des Moines, we learned that Black Hawk and part of his band had come and camped near the mouth of Devil Creek. I had some curiosity to see that famous old warrior, and Sullivan wanted to cheat some Indian out of a blanket or two, so we went together, walking about eight miles to the Indian lodges. I saw the famous Chief. He was a little old man at that time, with out paint, and dressed in part with white man's clothing, reticent[61], but not very dignified; but the scanty furniture about his Wick-a-up[62] was neat and clean. His squaw, for Black never had but one wife, was a paragon of neatness. His daughter was rather pretty. His sons were absent at that time.

We next went to the lodge of old Nottoway. He was an old acquaintance of Sullivan's and full of talk. I had a curiosity for knowledge, and got Sullivan to make enquiries for me of him. The old Indian became eloquent, but I could not understand a word at that time, and must give the story as Sullivan interpreted it to me.

The old Indian reached up both hands, spread out his fingers, slapped his hands together once, then stuck up one finger, then Sullivan said to me, Eleven years; keep still. The old

---

[61] Reserved, inhibited - not revealing one's thoughts or feelings readily
[62] Wickiup or Wigwam -

Indian talked and gesticulated[63] for some time. His squaw at one time made a vigorous gesture towards me saying, Chewaliski, Mani-ton, See-po. I was somewhat alarmed, thought she was going to strike me, but I afterwards learned that she was only giving emphasis to the name of the Creek. Eleven years back from that time would have made it about the year 1823, when most of the Indians lived near the mouth of Rock River, in Illinois. Quite a large party came down onto this creek to make she-se-pac (Shugar). Their sugar camps or boiling places extended several miles up the creek.

They had an excellent run for some three days, and still the sugar water kept running. The weather became sultry, even hot. A fog came on and seemed to hang in the trees near the surface of the ground, with occasional openings so they could see the clear sky above; yet there was occasional lightning on the underside of the fog, but no thunder. The fog grew thicker and the lightning increased in brightness, but still no

---

[63] use gestures, especially dramatic ones, instead of speaking or to emphasize one's words.

thunder could be heard. At last the earth began to tremble and a legion of devils came down the creek, riding on a big wave of water that stood up square in front, about ten feet high. The devils looked like balls of fire and run in every direction caught every Indian they could and carried them off bodily, as their remains were never found. They also carried off their kettles of syrup, hence the name, Chewaliski, Maniton, See-pa, or Evil-Spirit river; or in other words, Devil Creek.

This finishes the Indian legend. The probable facts in the case if there was any fact was that there was an extraordinary rain out on the head of the creek; that the lightning was where the rain was, but at such a distance that the Indians did not hear the thunder; and as the timber was dense, the Indians did not see the cloud in which the storm was, and the distance also made the lightning seem to be below the fog in their vicinity.

Now for the Devils. Every old settler knows how the Indians make sugar. It is by boiling the water a sap of the sugar maple in their copper kettles, hung on a pole, with the fire altogether on top of the ground, consuming a considerable quantity of wood crooked old logs and crooked sticks of all kinds are used.

Their fires were burning brightly; the rise in the creek come on suddenly, overflowing the banks, and floating off the logs. As they were already on fire, and as many of them were crooked, they remained with the fiery side up. The crooks in the creek made them seem to run in every direction, and a copper kettle, one third full of syrup, will float readily on the surface of the water, and may float many miles away.

Those few facts soberly considered will wipe out all the mysterious and superstitious portions of the story, and when simmered down it only amounts to this: the Indians took a big scare from a sudden rise in the creek; for they were a superstitious people.

This ends the play; but let us have the afterpiece. Superstition is not confined to the Indians alone. It is but some three or four years since there was a little excitement amongst the Baptist denomination of Christians in this vicinity. There were several candidates for the ordinance of baptism. Most of the converts objected to being baptized in Devil Creek. One young lady said she would rather risk her salvation without the saving ordinance than to be immersed in Devil Creek. So the preachers held a consultation and informed her that they had permanently changed the name from Devil Creek to Jordan. That made it all right, and she was immersed in Devil Creek.

Then, again, this creek will likely get on a rampage some other time and carry off some rails, and that will make those old farmers think of Devil Creek. So I go in for the old name of Devil Creek. The names of the young lady and the ministers are both withheld out of respect for their feelings.

Mr. Reed's account of Black Hawk

Mr Reed tells about the life, death and burial of Black Hawk - his neighbor and friend in the "Constitution-Democrat" on Oct. 6, 1903

I first met Black Hawk in the fall of 1837, five years after the battle of Bad Ax had ended the rebellion and after he had been taken on a tour of the eastern cities, to be impressed by the greatness of the country, after which he told his people that the white folks were as numerous as the leaves of the trees.

I remember very well the second time I ever saw Black Hawk. He was going to Fort Madison from his wick-a-up on Devil creek, about a mile from where my log cabin was. He was going for whisky.

Later in the day I saw him returning home, and although I knew he had been drinking practically all the day, he was walking as straight as a bee flies. He could drink an awful lot of whisky and never show any effects of it. When he came up opposite my cabin he crossed over and came in, saying he wanted to warm his moccasins. He was dressed peculiarly but rather customarily for him, wearing a fine broadcloth suit and a high silk hat, but he always wore moccasins; he has frequently told me that he could never stand the touch of hard leather on his feet, so he went everywhere in moccasins. It was to warm his moccasins that he stopped to see me that day. After he had been made comfortable my wife gave him a half of a mince pie and some coffee and he ate this with relish. When he was through he got ready to go on, after having thanked her for the food and complimenting it by saying "heap good." He said that his squaw would be waiting and watching for him and so he set off. Black Hawk was always a good man to his family.

After that we saw Black Hawk and his family very much. We were neighbors, only a mile distance between my cabin and his wick-a-up. I must say, too, that Black Hawk and his family were good neighbors. We didn't think anything of associating with Indians in those days; there were so many of them, they were as common as white folks today. We were not a bit afraid of them, either; we accepted them as a matter of course and got along fine. The fact that Black Hawk had been a great warrior and had gone on the warpath never bothered us. I don't recollect now that we ever thought much about it. Black Hawk was meek and peaceable in those days when I knew him.

When the government deposed him from being chief, after the war, and put Keokuk in his stead, Black Hawks spirit was broken. There was no danger from him any more. He became meek and mild, living out his remaining days as quietly as possible.

I can recall very well how the chief looked in those days. He was rather small in stature and very slight when I knew him, not weighing much over 125 pounds. He was bald and kind of dried up or shriveled, as though the sorrows and troubles he had had withered him like an old leaf. Around his own wick-a-up he always wore a blanket and moccasins, but when he went out he usually wore either a uniform or broadcloth suit and silk hat. He always wore moccasins.

While the chief himself was a slight, frail, old man, his son, Nes-se-as-kuk, was as fine a specimen of manhood as I ever saw, with splendid physique, and broad chested, standing five feet, eleven inches high, and weighing fully 190 pounds.

Madam Black Hawk was a very fine looking woman,

much lighter in color than most Indians. I always had the idea that she was part French, to judge from her appearance.

Black Hawk had another son, the settlers called him Tom Black Hawk. He was a bad Indian and hated the whites bitterly.

Aside from the old chief, interest in those days in the family centered in the daughter, Nauasia, the prettiest Indian girl I ever saw in my life, a girl of such striking beauty that she would attract attention anywhere. Nauasia was the belle of the settlements those days. The white folks said her name was an Indian corruption of Nancy.

After a year or two of living in Fort Madison a couple of hotels were built, and it was our custom to have frequent balls. Nauasia was the belle every time. Not a young white fellow but would give almost anything he had for the honor of a dance with Nauasia. And what a dancer! She was as spry and agile as a fawn. I never saw a girl lighter on her feet than Nauasia. The young fellows would stand around and look eagerly until they mustered up courage to ask her for a dance, and then everybody envied them. Nauasia was a mighty graceful dancer. She would leap high in the air and whirl around and cut fancy capers until she had beaten every other dancer in the settlement. There was quite a romance in Nauasia's life. Some young fellow came out from New York and fell desperately in love with her. Nauasia loved him, too, and they were to be married. But the young man's folks back east heard of it and ordered him home at once. I suppose they thought she was just a common Indian squaw. But she was not, by any means. And the desertion of her lover pretty near broke Nauasia's heart.

I have several times been a guest in the Black Hawk wick-a-up. It was quite a large wick-a-up, with space for the entire family and one room which was given over entirely to Black Hawk's relics and possessions. I have counted no less than twelve large leather trunks which Black Hawk had after his trip through the east. I never saw into these trunks, but there was good reason for me to believe that they were filled with mementoes of his trip.

The Black Hawks usually spent the winter in Lee County, and just as soon as sugar making was over in the spring they would pull up and go somewhere else. I remember being in the Black Hawk home one time when Madam Black Hawk was making sugar and she gave me a large mould of sugar to take home with me.

As I said before, there was not much thought in those days of the war Black Hawk had headed. He had been defeated and deposed and his spirit had been so broken that he was looked on as a harmless old man.

As to the war itself, the prime cause was the plowing up of the Indian's corn fields and graveyards in their big village up at Rock Island. An Indians' burial ground is sacred to them, and when the whites came in and plowed up their bones and planted corn in their graves they were furious. Then the whites plainly violated the terms of the treaties and took land that wasn't theirs. The war was really forced on the Indians. I never thought they were very much to blame. The war had a disastrous termination. At the battle of Bad Ax, men and women and little children were fired on and brutally murdered. The spirit of the Indians was forever crushed after that.

While Mr. Reed was best acquainted with Black Hawk by reason of having been a near neighbor, he was also familiar with the other noted Indians of the time, notably Keokuk and Wapello. In regard to these chiefs he said:

"Keokuk, Wapello and Hardfish were made chiefs of the tribe by the government after Black Hawk had been deposed. I saw them all, Keokuk several times. Keokuk was the only blue-eyed Indian I ever saw. He was a much larger man than Black Hawk, rather fat and pompous. He was nothing much but a gambler and a horse racer. Those were the only things he cared for. He was a hard drinker, but I want to say right here that neither Keokuk or Black Hawk were drunkards."

Keokuk had four wives and Black Hawk only one. When Keokuk became chief in place of Black Hawk the majority of the tribe followed him. But until the day of his death Black Hawk had a large following which was faithful to him and still regarded him as the chief.

Black Hawk was not living at his wick-a-up in Lee County when he died, but higher up, near Iowaville. I had not seen him for several months before his death, but three months after he died I saw his body where it had been placed in a shack or grave at the upper end of the prairie near Iowaville, in Davis County. The body had been placed in the shack or pen which was about 18X15 feet in size. At his side was placed the cane which Henry Clay had given him. A number of his relics were also placed near him. Outside the pen was a post, about fifteen feet high, on which was painted in red paint the pictures of the animals Black Hawk had killed in his lifetime.

Three months after the burial I went to the pen and lifting up a board at the corner looked in, saw the chief, the cane and the things that were buried with him. A few months later somebody in Cincinnati stole the body, to exhibit it, I guess, and the Indians raised an awful fuss. The government took the matter in charge and finally brought a skeleton and put it in the pen where Black Hawk had been buried. The Indians were pacified, but I have always felt sure that the body reburied was not the body of Black Hawk at all.

The body was placed on the surface of the ground in a sitting posture, with the face toward the southeast, and the body supported in that position by a wooden slab or puncheon. On his left side was placed a cane given him by Henry Clay, with his right hand resting upon it. He was dressed in a full military suit, which had been presented to him by President Jackson. Three silver medals hung upon his breast, all of which had been presented to him by distinguished persons during his visits to Washington. There were also placed in the grave two swords, an extra pair of moccasins, and some other articles of Indian costume, with a sufficient supply of provisions to last him three days on the journey to the spirit land. Around the body and the articles buried with it were two large blankets closely wrapped. Two wooden forks were then firmly driven in the ground, and a pole placed upon them extending over the body. The whole was then covered with sod to the depth of about one foot. At his feet, a flagstaff was placed, floating a beautiful silk American flag, which had been presented to him. The flag remained over his grave until the winds tore it to pieces and long after the body had disappeared. A post was planted by the grave, on which was inscribed, or painted, some figures commemorative of his deeds. Subsequently his relatives and friends enclosed the grave with a rude picket fence, and fondly hoped that the remains of the great was chief were at rest.

One morning about July 1, 1839, Black Hawk's bereaved widow returned from her accustomed visit to his grave bitterly weeping. Calling on Mr. Jordan, she informed him that some one had opened the grave and taken away the head of her husband. Mr.

Jordan promised to do all that he could to find out who had taken it. The next winter the rest of the skeleton disappeared. It afterward transpired that one Dr. Turner, who lived at Lexington, a little village at that time situated just above the present town of Bonaparte, in Van Buren County, was the man who had committed the deed. He came in the night and attempted to seize the body, but being frightened only succeeded in getting the head, which he carried away in his saddlebags. The next winter he came again and carried off the rest of the skeleton. They were conveyed to Quincy, Ill., where the different parts were united with wire. Black Hawk's relatives complained bitterly at the outrage. Finally the man in Quincy to whom Dr. Turner had delivered the remains, informed Governor Lucas of Iowa that he would hold them subject to his order. The governor directed that they be forwarded to his office in Burlington and on the receipt of them informed Black Hawk's relatives of the fact. His two sons immediately proceeded to Burlington, where they saw the skeleton in the executive office. They were afraid, however, that if they brought it home with them, it might again be stolen and concluding that the governor's office was the safest and best place for it they left it there. At the expiration of his official term, Governor Lucas delivered the skeleton over to his successor, Governor Chambers. It was finally placed in a museum which was established in Burlington and some years after, with many other valuable and curious relics which had been collected, was consumed by fire.

Black Hawk as an Elder

This description of Black Hawk was printed in "The Gate City" on Aug. 1, 1880.

The Former Indian Chiefs life and Death in Iowa

The Davenport Democrat, in an article on Early History," says of Black Hawk's appearance at the last treaty made: "At this treaty Black Hawk was present, but was allowed to have no part in the proceedings, but stood apart with his warrior son, Nan-she-as-kuk, and a few other friends as sad, sullen, silent spectators. It was the last visit made by the valiant old chief to this locality - his most loved home - the home of his fathers and tribe for many hundred years. In token of his supreme disgust for Indian patriotism and Indian recreancy[64] under Keokuk, he had thrown off his Indian garb - breaches and blanket changed for a pair of dingy gray pants and black broad-cloth frock-coat, moccasins for cowhide boots war Paint washed off, hair grown out, scalp lock removed - the whole surmounted by a tall narrow-rimmed, much-battered, drab-colored hat, and in his hand a cane - presenting on the whole a - most grotesque and ludicrous appearance. The proud old king had become an outcast and dejected, he repaired to the Des Moines, on the banks of which, near Iowaville, in Wapello County, he died on October 3rd, 1838. His bones, which were some years after placed in the historical society rooms in Burlington, were consumed by the fire which destroyed the building which contained them.

---

[64] Cowardly actions

How the Indians Counted and Pioneer Life

A description of Indian words and settler life including door usage, the latch string, and meat curing is related in the Feb 3rd, 1898 issue of "The Daily Gate City."

Birmingham Enterprise: We learned many Indian words, and could talk with them very well. When they became excited enough to swear they always used the English words, having no profane words in their vocabulary. They had only ten in counting. When they wanted to tell how old anything was, they held up both hands with the fingers spread-that meant ten. If it should happen to be twenty-four, they would put up both hands twice and then four fingers - that many snows or winters. They counted ten in this manner: Goat, wish, sway, neum, neumnome, nowatsocowatso, goatawatso, shaw, quick. I will give you a few of their names for different things: Cocus - hog; nucatucashaw - horse; scotch - fire; napawnee - flour; mishanoby papoose - a boy; fish - water; succotash - corn and beans; massages - rattle snakes.

The Pottawattamie tribe passed through Birmingham, Iowa territory, when they moved west.

The Black Hawk Indians were large fine looking men, six feet high, well proportioned; some of the females were handsome, fine looking women.

In 1837 the Black Hawk tribe made a settlement on the Des Moines River, where Iowaville now is. He and his two sons and daughters settled there. The old man died Oct. 3, 1838. His two sons used to come into this neighborhood to trade with the settlers. We would buy buckskins of them. They used to call at fathers and could talk English very well. The earlier settlers in Iowa all lived in log cabins, and after we got to raising hogs, the Kentuckians would dig out large troughs and put under the beds to cure their meat in. We learned to live very economical on our corn bread and bacon. When visitors came it was customary to have sweetened corn bread and that was considered extra fine. Orleans molasses was used to sweeten everything. The cabin doors were hung on wooden hinges and when company came they could be taken off and laid down, and answered the double purpose of dining tables. You have often heard the remark, "Our latch-string is always out; come and see us." The latch and ketch in those days were made of wood; the latch had a string tied to it, a hole made through the door just above the latch, one end of the string put through the hole and hung outside. When outside you pulled the string to unlatch it; at night the string was pulled inside. That locked the door to outsiders.

The Great Indian Battle of Iowaville

A.W. Harlan tells the account of the slaughter of the Ioway Indians by Black Hawk as given by Pashepaho, 2nd in command to Black Hawk in the Jan. 17, Jan 27 and Feb 3 1874 issues of "The Daily Gate City."

Mr. Editor: I hold it to be a duty of man while in life to leave a record of passing events both for the amusement and instruction of those that may come on the stage of life after us. This I think should be termed a second-hand narrative. I would not vouch that it possesses sufficient authenticity to be termed history, and I flatter myself that it may contain more truth than is usually embodied in a legend.

The reader will please bear in mind that wonderful changes have occurred in this western country within from forty to sixty years. Fifty years ago we had but few steamboats and no railroads or telegraph lines, and but few newspapers in circulation. The local news was circulated by neighborhood gossips.

Travelers, though strangers to each other when meeting on the highway, generally passed a few words, giving each other the news from more distant localities. Neighbors visited frequently and the evenings were often passed by listening to hunting stories, and hair-breadth escapes from Indians in war times on the frontiers. Most of the people on the frontier could neither read nor write, but many of them had a tolerable faculty for telling a yarn. I have hesitated about giving this narrative, knowing that I should differ from some others who had heard but few of the particulars.

It has been almost forty years since Giles O. Sullivan settled where Bentonsport, Van Buren county, Iowa is now situated. The writer hereof was located a little above that place, and at that time the frontier Settler, some Indian traders only being still further up the Des Moines.

Pashepaho, meaning when translated into English, the Stabbing Chief, chanced to be passing that way and called upon his old friend Sullivan to enjoy the hospitalities of his cabin. Sullivan knew that I had a little whisky, and perhaps may have been a little dry himself, so he sent for me to come down and fetch some liquor and have a sociable chat with old Pashepaho.

Sullivan had always lived on the frontier of Missouri and spoke the Indian language better than many of the traders. As to my part I knew but a few words of the language, but then I felt a more lively interest in hearing their history and adventures.

PASHEPAHO, THE STABBER

Now let me describe Pashepaho; He was at that time about fifty years of age, with the Greek profile, a little below medium height, remarkably well muscled, though a little inclined to corpulency[65], very large head, and an indescribably something in his eyes that was not easily forgotten. He spoke but seldom when duly sober, but with a moderate amount of stimulus was quite communicative. Sullivan's Indian name was Muscoet-ipaw, or Red Whiskers. My Indian name was sow-wow-wiskanoo, or Yellow Bird. Henry Plummer and Pe-she-ma-na-po, or O.P. Thomas formed the little audience before whom Pashepaho between dram narrated many bloody scenes in his life and as he occasionally paused in the narrative, Sullivan interpreted what he had been saying to us. Sullivan first made enquiries about the battle of Sink Hole. This was a fight between Black Hawk or Mack-I lak mish-I kah kack[66] and a few rangers somewhere in Pike or Lincoln counties, Missouri, before those counties were organized. Then Pashepaho gave the particulars

---

[65] To be overweight
[66] Black Hawk's name is pronounced Ma-ka-tai-me-she-kia-kiak today

of a battle with the Osage Indians near the mouth of Honey Creek and I believe within the present bounds of Clark County, Missouri in which they defeated the Osage with little loss to the Sauk and Fox Indians.

Pashepaho was a sub-chief under Black Hawk and almost always with him. He was a spectator of the battle between Barclay and Perry in the last British war. His description was amusing. He says that Barclay said it would only be a breakfast spell to whip that boy. The result, of course, was rather disgusting to him. At last it seems to have had rather a demoralizing effect on their Indian allies, as most of them left and came in to near the mouth of Rock River in Illinois.

The united bands of Sauk and Fox Indians had long held sway[67] in the country east of the Mississippi, and as far north as Green Bay, and even to Lake Superior, having previously whipped and then made friends of the Winnebagoes and Monemonees and frequently ranging as far south as St. Louis.

The Sioux occupied most of the present State of Minnesota and the country to the northwest. With these the Sauk and Fox had many bloody battles, but I never heard of their making friends.

The Igh-ho-was, or Ioways, had for many years occupied just about the whole country that now forms the State of Iowa. They were a proud and warlike nation, and between them and the Sauk and Fox for many years war had existed as a pastime. But from 1815 until May, 1823, it was war to the knife and the knife to the hilt, literally and not theoretically.

Up to 1815 the Igh-ho-was had their principal villages on the Iowa River, but their inveterate and ever-wakeful enemy Black Hawk, harassed them so in his many daring forays[68] that they were compelled to move on to the Des Moines; their principal village being situated just where Iowaville now stands, and even here Black Hawk, Pashepaho, and a few followers, less than fifty in all, well mounted men made a dash into their

---

[67] Having a controlling interest
[68] Raids or sudden attacks.

village in 1818, killing a great many, and making good their retreat to Illinois with but little loss to themselves. But it must be borne in mind that the Igh-ho-was, in personal prowess and bravery, were not a whit[69] their inferiors, and they, in turn, often carried the war far into Illinois, returning with many scalps of their enemies and holding their war dances in return. But they lacked a leader; at least such a leader as Black Hawk, for if the simile may be allowed, Black Hawk was the great napoleon of the savages, and Pashepaho was something more of a Marshal Ney and a Murat to him.

Thus matters stood until the Fall of 1822 when a small part of Black Hawk's band were encamped near where Montrose is situated, a small party of Igh-ho-was[70] braves were out on the war path they came upon a few squaws of the Sauks and maltreated them in such a way that is seldom forgiven by any nation of people. The deed was not approved by of a majority of their nation, but they could not apologize. Blood only could atone[71] for such enormity of sins, and both nations prepared for the terrible ordeal. Now let it be borne in mind that each party could raise an equal number of warriors, say about 200 on each side, but as their principal towns were situated just about as Washington and Richmond were during our late unpleasantness, prudence seems to have suggested the policy to both parties of keeping near one-half of their braves to guard their homes.

There is one thing more that should be borne in mind, and that is that Black Hawk had taken lessons in war of able British Generals and understood the value of a navy, and therefore provided himself with more and better canoes than any of the neighboring nations possessed. This enabled him to move almost unmolested amongst enemies for hundreds of miles and he may have had some advantage in fire arms, but at that time most of the Indian fighting was done with bows and arrows, the arrow having a steel point generally of British manufacture.

---

[69] A very small part of amount
[70] Ioway tribe – alternate spelling
[71] make amends or reparation

The gross insult was perpetrated so late in the fall that it could not be avenged immediately as most of the Indians were scattered on their fall hunt. Instead of immediate war, Black Hawk, in council, recommended laying up an extra supply of dried venison and elk meat and giving it in charge of

certain chiefs to be kept for a special grand campaign in the spring following. He did not permit any small war parties to leave any of his villages. But he increased the number of his scouts or spies with special orders to not disturb the enemy in any way if possible, to avoid collision and only take a scalp rather than loose one. The Igh-ho-was from the same motives adopted the same policy as to the spies, but neglected to provide the extra dried venison or commissary stores. Thus both countries were traversed by their enemies, spies unmolested and all seemed serene and quiet. But it was only the calm that precedes the storm. Spring had opened early; both parties had made She-se-pac or sugar in peace. The trees' were leafing out beautifully. The squaws of both nations were hunting up their rusty hoes and looking to their Tom-i-noch or seed corn, mus-co-chees[72], &c[73], preparing for raising the usual

---

[72] Squash or pumpkin
[73] Type set for etc. or &

summer crop. The braves of both nations were, uneasy and restless as some of their scouts returned almost daily and reported the situation: even the squaws and children, especially the Skin-e-way, or boys, seemed to feel that a crisis was approaching. And yet the sun shone as warm, and the grass grew as beautiful, on the banks of the Des Moines, as it ever did in Eden or any other spot on God's earth.

About this time a larger body of the Igh-ho-was than usual went on a spring hunt. Meat was wanted for the Pick-a-ninnies, or small children, as well as for a grand contemplated expedition towards Black Hawk's town, near the mouth of Rock River, in Illinois. They took nearly all their canoes and many of their best horses or nack-a-lo-ka-shees. Some of Black Hawk's spies saw them fairly under way and reported in haste. Others watched the expedition as far as the mouth of White Breast, and then reported, and yet some two or three still remained to watch for further developments.

Their hunt was a grand success. Elk and buffalo in abundance were slain in a short time; the canoes were loaded; the river was in a beautiful stage, say about 9 feet above low water mark. They made good time to their village; all hands were engaged in drying or jerking meat and having a general feast.

Their mounted men had returned their horses in good condition; grass was abundant; almost the whole nation was assembled; the details were being made for one grand foray, as well as for home guards, and as the sun rose beautiful, several hundred Igh-ho-was were out on the prairie trying the speed of their horses, but without arms of any kind. To them everything looked lovely and the goose hung high.

Now let us learn what Black Hawk, the famous war chief of the Sauk and Fox nations, was about. Black Hawk started on a spring hunt near the same time that the Iowas had done so. He knew that his every move was watched by Iowa spies. He took many canoes and ponies with him, much as the Iowas had done. He went some thirty or forty miles up Rock River and scattered for a general hunt, but with special orders to hunt and slay all the Iowa spies and return to a certain place in two days.

His orders were promptly obeyed; most, if not all the spies were killed, and a reasonable amount of venison procured, and at dusk all were ready to embark[74] on the canoes for the village. Those that were mount had quietly moved south, and at a certain time were to meet the war party on the Mississippi a little above Nauvoo. The party in the canoes or Ghe-mans, made all possible haste to the village, left their fresh meat and took on a sufficient supply of dried venison saved over from the previous hunt, with some parched corn and all their war implements, and without a moment's rest proceed on their way down the Mississippi. While part of the crew of each canoe wielded their paddles others slept as best they could. Thus they moved with wonderful speed all night long, and near dawn of day had reached some Islands below the mouth of the Iowa River. Here they quietly moved into a small slough between two Islands; the men got out, and, after placing a few pickets[75] where they could have a good outlook while they themselves were concealed. The whole body, some nine hundred warriors slept through the day so quietly that an army of white men would have passed on either side of the river without a suspicion of their presence.

The next night and within a few hours they had reached the place above Nauvoo where the Calvary portion of the expedition was to meet them. Each party had come to the time as agreed. The lashings for the canoes were all ready, and in this way most of the horses were ferried over at night, and before the dawn they were all quietly resting in the woods near the mouth of Devil Creek, a few miles below Fort Madison, and here for another day a death-like stillness pervaded; all rested and refreshed, as night came on, they took up their line of march, or rather an Indian lope[76], for as day dawned they were near Iowaville, a distance of full fifty miles. Though it was still dark, they knew just about where to find the vedettes[77]

---

[74] To begin a course of action
[75] Soldiers performing a specific function
[76] Long smooth bounding stride- similar to trot of horse
[77] mounted sentry beyond outposts to observe enemy movements

of the Iowas, and had kindly cared for them by taking off their scalps.

Pashepaho with about fifty well mounted men had gone on to the highlands Northeast of Iowaville, to find a favorable location and await events, whilst Black Hawk and several other chiefs of various grades were to keep in the timber near the bank of the Des Moines and make an impetuous[78] attack on the Iowa lodges and drive them out into the open prairie where the mounted men could, with tomahawk in hand, make a successful charge.

Just here in the narrative Pashepaho got rather dry; Sullivan gave me the wink and we all liquored, and while Pashepaho takes his wind let me tell you how the land lies, or how it used to lie thereabouts.

Below Iowaville about Independent[79], was a large body of timber running up the river to a point a little sharper than a sad iron; near the upper end of said timber, and in the edge of the prairie, was a number of bark lodges. Then for more than half a mile the prairie comes near the river with some low land intervening covered with cottonwood, young willows and grape vines, forming a dense undergrowth.

Old Pashepaho has taken his breath, let us hear him: He and his party were concealed in a hollow; all was quiet; some delay had occurred with the main body as he thought. The sun rose, and instead of a sleeping village, his eyes beheld about two thousand Igh-ho-was braves, many of them painted, running foot races as well as horse racing on the prairie. He looked on for a short time; concluded that Black Hawk would not attack against such odds, but, seeing that they had no arms with them, he concluded to make a dash as him and some others had done five years before.

They mounted their ponies; some old grass that stood in a wet place and had not been burned, hid them for a time, and almost

---

[78] quickly without thought or care
[79] Now called Selma, IA

before the Igh-ho-was knew of his presence he was cleaving their scalps with the tomahawk.

The yells that usually follow such an attack may be heard for miles. I have no language at command to describe such scenes. Some hundred and fifty or two hundred Igh-ho-was were, slain in less than five minutes, and Pashepaho and his small party were in full retreat down the prairie towards their main body, and in less than twenty minutes some hundreds of Iowas were mounted, well armed, and in pursuit of them.

In the meantime the main body of Sauks and Foxes, under the command of Black Hawk, had hastened up the river bank through the timber and attacked the nearest lodges and burned them. This, of course, produced another grand commotion. The Iowas ceased their pursuit of Pashepaho and his party and returned for the defense of their village, one-third of which was already burned, and their old enemies were well posted in the timber, where the lay of the land gave them an important advantage, with the river to protect their rear and furnish them a supply of water.

In the meantime Pashepaho had joined the main party. Hostilities ceased for a little while. Each party held a council of war. Many of the Foxes were for returning home, but Black Hawk said he had come to fight it out with the Igh-ho-was, even if there were more than two to one of them. Then Pashepaho said Black Hawk was angry with him for making the attack in the way he did, before the others were ready.

Black Hawk soon arranged his plans. His position was good for several days. He would at least fight one day in his present position, and if necessary he could spare a large party to swim the river in the night and attack the Iowa camps in the rear at dawn of day. This may look rather desperate in the face of such a foe. Such ventures if unsuccessful are a lasting disgrace; but when successful they bring immortal renown. So it proved in this case. There is a time in almost every well contested battle that the final result depends on the bravery of less than a half dozen subordinates, as for instance the battle of Pea Ridge.

But let us have the story as I heard it from Pashepaho himself. After saying that Black Hawk was angry with him for his rash attack so early in the morning, he said Black Hawk told him to take a few men, swim the river and carefully search for Igh-ho-was vedettes and kill all of them; this was to prepare for contingencies. Old Pashepaho took but two men that had been scouts, one a mere boy, went down the river about a mile, waded in and swam over cool as it was. We will leave him in search of picket posts while we engage in detailing an unusual mode of Indian fighting.

The system adopted by both parties was the result of circumstances and not from a love of display or from generosity or fairness. The tactics of each party was to induce the other to make a rash attack and thus expose themselves to much loss. Both parties had some firearms, though nearly all the fighting through the day was done with bows and arrows, each Indian having only one bow and quiver - that is a kind of stick made of raw hide, containing a number of arrows slightly fastened on the inside so that when one arrow is discharged the warrior can readily seize and in a remarkably short time discharge another arrow. I believe it is a little ahead of the old Allen revolver. Black Hawk next sent a small party with supports in their rear to examine and if possible approach the enemy in that direction. They met some Igh-ho-was pickets, did a little fighting and returned to the main body and reported the route impracticable.

Black Hawk then sent out a small party of about 20 men under command of some young brave that wanted to distinguish himself. The Igh-ho-was promptly sent out exactly the same number to meet them. They fought in the open prairie, where there was nothing to screen them as there usually is in most Indian fighting. The old grass having been burned, the new; grass had scarcely grown. The fight lasted some considerable time. Most of both parties were slain. A few of each party returned with scalps.

Then a small body of men sallied[80] forth from each party to succor[81] the wounded that were left on the ground, and save them from being scalped by the enemy. This was usually the most interesting part of the game; for it tried their strength as well as their bravery and horsemanship, one single Indian often picking up a wounded comrade, throwing him on his horse, then mounting himself and getting safely off from the field among a flight of well-directed arrows.

The ground being fairly cleared of the dead, the Igh-ho-was opened the frolic by sending out about thirty braves in the panoply[82] of war - that is, almost naked - but most fantastically painted up with white clay, yellow ochre and vermillion, sometimes bearing a strong resemblance to a Bengal tiger.

Of course they were promptly met by an exactly equal number from the opposing party, all armed with bows and arrows. The fight was only a repetition of the one just described, and thus for several hours the fight continued, the mass of both parties looking on, idle, but much interested spectators.

On some occasions the Igh-ho-was did not exactly come to time; then the Sauk and Fox would show many antics, give gestures of defiance, make most insulting, and, I might add, obscene exposure of their persons in full view of the Iowa squaws, but often lost their scalps for their impudence[83] a few minutes afterwards. Thus the two parties, when of equal number in open ground, are just about as well matched as the famous Killkeny cats.

So just let them fight on and let us remember that every lick that brings down a savage promotes civilization.

And now for a little while let us follow the fortunes of Pashepaho. Now comes a tough yarn. I do not ask anybody to believe all of it, for I did not fully believe it myself at the time, and then you have it cheaper than I got it; for it cost me two

---

[80] a military sortie - sudden rush
[81] Give assistance or aid
[82] Splendid display
[83] Rash or without considering consequences

jorums[84] of liquor and had like to have got me into serious difficulty next morning.

Pashepaho and his two comrades cautiously approach unobserved the first picket post; the two Indians are intently watching the frolic on the other side of the river while three well directed arrows have pierced their vitals; one falls, dead without any noise, but the other gave an unearthly yell before he expired. That yell was heard by the vedettes at another picket post, and they were on the alert, met their enemy in the brush and gave them nearly half of it, killing one of them and seriously wounding the other one, but old Pashepaho, with his usual luck, was unhurt; he resolved to continue the fight alone; he reached the woods faithfully but found no other enemies; he had a good view of everything on the other side of the river; carefully noted the position of the picket posts among the bushes; looked on at leisure. He soon perceived that if those pickets under the bank were destroyed they could attain an easy victory over the enemy.

He then resolved to do or die alone, and went up the river some distance, and, behind the shelter of a grape vine. He was meditating. Just then a forked log floating down stream caught among the vines at his feet. It was just what he wanted. He left his bow and arrows, and with his, tomahawk and scalping knife in his belt, he took to the water taking the leg with him and keeping his head concealed between the  forks, and in this way crossed the river without being observed. He landed exactly where he wished to do, but in landing a grape vine caught his tomahawk and pulled it from his belt and slightly shook the vine. This attracted the attention of the Indian at that post, he looked around carefully; cut the grape vine that held the forked log.; it only swung in nearer the bank and held fast, and really favored him. His knife only was left.

---

[84] Large jug or bowl for serving liquor

He crept under the vines as far as he dared to do. Some yell of exultation[85] out on the prairie attracted the attention of that Igh-ho-was. He looked that way and Pashepaho's knife reached his heart. His bleeding scalp was soon on the belt with two others from over the river; his tomahawk was just what Pashepaho needed most at that particular time.

His friendly log lay near; he carefully crawled under and into the fork again, and steadily floated down to the next picket post. The brush and Vines again favored his landing, but here were two Indians; but his Tomahawk was all right. They were intently watching the performances out on the Prairie and the first intimation[86] they had of his presence was the sound of the tomahawk in one of their skulls, but somehow it stuck; it took the second jerk to get it loose and by that time the other Indian had drawn his tomahawk; a few terrible blows were struck and parried by both parties and somehow the handle of his tomahawk was broken, the other man's Tomahawk flew out of his hand; the scalping knife comes next, and Pashepaho was soon victorious as he has so often been before, add two additional Scalps soon dangled from his belt.

The tomahawk of his enemy now graces his belt, but no whoop of exultation escapes him; he remembers there is still one more picket post to pass. His guardian angel whispers to him, caution; he felt that the success of the whole enterprise rested on him just then, and never before or afterwards did he feel so great a responsibility. But it must be done. He carefully crawled into the fork of his favorite log, floated down slowly near the bank, stopping a little above the post; he crawled cut, breathed a moment, weighed the importance of the next few moments. He felt fatigued; he was chilled going in and out of the water frequently; he knew the next minute would immortalize him with his people or leave him only dead Injun. Again a yell of indignation went up from his friends on the prairie; one of the vedettes moved a few feet to get a better view of the frolic and he cleft the skull of the other. The next

---

[85] Triumphant yell of joy.
[86] indication or hint

moment he had to parry a well aimed blow from the last savage; he proved to be a powerful man; the contest was long and doubtful; at length both tomahawks went whizzing away; the knife ended the contest in favor of Pashepaho, and with seven scalps in his belt he again took to his log; went below their own lines and landed. Then as you might say, he went to headquarters feeling proud. Threw down his seven scalps, made a short report, told Black Hawk the way was open under the river bank. Black Hawk turned his eyes to keshuswe - the sun; it was 4 o'clock. The last contest on the prairie had ended slightly in their favor. A lively commotion ensued Two hundred men were ordered to form in line on the prairie and a still larger number including all those with provisions were to proceed in haste up through the brush on the river bank, and make a savage attack to the rear of the Igh-ho-was, and yet another line of near 200 men, formed in the rear of those already out on the prairie. This of course, called out an equal number of Ioway's and weakened their guard next the river. This had just occurred when old Pashepaho came out of the brush and attacked the rear with great impetuosity[87]; and with fearful yells and the keen cracking of more than one hundred guns, it is no wonder that a general panic ensued among the Igh-ho-was. Their Chiefs comprehended the situation. Their four hundred braves, then in line, first became motionless, then wavered and fell back in confusion. The rout[88] became complete. Most of Pashepaho's party mounted themselves on horses that seemed to have been just hitched up for their special use, and all they had to do was to keep in line and hew the retreating Igh-ho-was on the head as they run. A few jumped into the river and swam over; others reached their canoes and were shot while crossing over and others escaped by keeping in the brush. Night closed the scene.

The proud Igh-ho-was as a nation were wiped out; and not even a whoop of exultation was heard from the conquerors; and but few warriors of established reputation even

---

[87] Having or marked by violent force
[88] disorderly retreat of defeated troops

condescended to take a scalp. A few of the boys took many scalps. Pashepaho said from the time he threw down those seven scalps that day he had never taken a scalp. The Sauk and Foxes slept quietly that night.

The remains of the Igh-ho-was congregated over near Soap Creek, but only one of their chiefs of any note had survived, and I have forgotten his name. He sent over a flag of truce. Peace was made, and they were permitted to bury their dead without molestation. The terms of peace were entirely of Black Hawk's dictation. He told them that all former differences were rubbed out. Their former hunting grounds should be held in common and if they wished at any time thereafter, they could become a part of his nation. In this one battle the Sauk and Fox Indians acquired all the title that our government got from them in the several treaties, but just here let me record the fact to the credit of Hardfish and young Nash-eas-kuk, Black Hawk's oldest son, that on the last treaty, when they sold all their lands in Iowa, they went up the Missouri River, hunted up all they could find of that once powerful tribe, say about 250, rather disconsolate[89] looking human beings and insisted that they should share in the payments in the proportion of their numbers. Keokuk and other chiefs could not see things in that light; neither could the agent Mr. Beach. They left the agency, wandered away, may have mixed with the wild tribes on the plains, but since the fall of 1842 I have not heard of them as a people. I shall endeavor to add a few observations to illustrate what I have already written. I have endeavored to so write this narrative as to leave the same impression on the mind of the reader that it did on my mind when I first heard it from Pashepaho himself. Though I have heard nearly all the particulars rehearsed by other braves at their war dance, I never felt the same interest as the first.

After the old chief had finished his narrative and I learned the meaning of the name Pashepaho or Stabbing Chief, I had Sullivan inquire what his name had been previous to that time.

---

[89] Cheerless or unhappy

He readily gave some jaw-breaking name that I did not remember for a day. He informed us that he had risen from obscurity by his own deeds of daring, and that his present proud title of the Stabbing Chief was given to him by Black Hawk next day after the battle of Iowaville for his deeds of daring and remarkable success in the use of the knife, and was universally concurred in and never disputed.

Comments on the Indian Battle at Iowaville

A follow-up on the battle by A.W. Harlan in "The Daily Gate City" on Feb. 10, 1874

In the spring of 1835, just twelve years from the time the battle was fought, and after I had heard all the particulars, the Indians met on the ground to have a celebration. I was not present on that occasion, and first learned some of the particulars from William Avery and Henry Netherton, who were present and saw the whole performance, and as a climax or closing scene, Keokuk led out his finest horse having on his finest trappings, and offered him as a premium to any one that could give the most forcible illustration of the antics and obscene gestures with which they had bantered the Igh-ho-was on the day of the battle. Five young braves entered the list to compete. The play was most exhilarating to those cultivated savages, and the horse and trappings were actually awarded, for the edifying[90] display.

I see that I have neglected to name one little incident: I had Sullivan enquire of Pashepaho how he had so often escaped being killed. He said the Good Spirit always stood between him and his enemies, and took a table cloth of Mrs. Sullivan's, spread it up before him, and showed us how their knives and tomahawks would glance off, but he also exhibited some ugly scars where they had not entirely glanced off.

I notice in looking over the manuscript that I had neglected to say that all those picket posts under the river bank had been provided with fire arms in case of attack that their reports might give the alarm, but such had been the sudden and unexpected attack of Pashepaho that not a single gun had been fired. I also think it would be nothing to make a few comments.

---

[90] providing moral or intellectual instruction

There is but few Iowa soldiers that may read this narrative but would at once ask, why did not the Igh-ho-was divide their forces and attack Black Hawk in the rear. I can only say in reply that they had no chief that was a General Sherman to lead them. They could have divided their forces and marched down in the open prairie, and if attacked, it would have been as fair as the fighting they were doing all day long. And if they could have reached the timber in his rear, would really have had the advantage and could probably have wiped out Black Hawk's whole force in two hours. Then any one could have seen what a fool Black Hawk was to get himself in such a trap. Such is the glorious uncertainty of war.

It is the bold move, indomitable[91] courage and perseverance that make the hero.

I see that I have used the phrase "war for pastime."

War amongst savages is the only road to distinction. And the Shushkese or young women are an article of trade, and rate in price from one or two up to ten horses each. The Skin-e-way or young man must raise them in some way before he can marry. Indeed, he is scarcely treated with ordinary respect by the braves until he has taken a scalp. But when he has gone on a foray and returned with a scalp a sudden change comes over all his acquaintances; the finest apparel is loaned or given to him; his face is newly painted, his head is festooned most fantastically with fine shavings from some soft wood; a new dance is inaugurated; he is, after a time, invited to make his maiden speech and tell with what grace he stripped off the first scalp, and then, if all is approved, he is allowed the inestimable privilege of wearing the tail of a skunk tied to his leggins[92]. Then, as the young warrior walks through the village the observed of all observers, many of those olive colored, maidens that would have scarcely spoken to him ten days before often come in his way with their faces apparently veiled, but not quite half concealed. And a

---

[91] Incapable of being overcome, subdued, or vanquished; unconquerable
[92] buckskin leg coverings

Shushkese that would have cost him at least ten horses ten days before, he can now buy for one or two horses, and if the maiden reciprocates the gentle passion, she will prevail on some of her friends to give him a chance to win the horses in a foot race.

Horrible Indian Depredations in Iowa

In the – Apr. 26, 1857 issue of "The Keokuk Daily Post," W. Williams. Reports on the military actions after the Spirit Lake Massacre. This occurred 10 years after the settling of Pella, IA

Sixty persons murdered, wounded and missing!

We have had, for several weeks past, rumors of burnings of settlements and murderings of settlers in Northern and North-Western Iowa, by the Indians, but nothing definite and reliable has come before the public, until the following official communication which we are permitted to copy. It will be seen that the accounts already published have fallen short of the reality, which is of the most startling character. Something should be done for the protection of frontier settlements from future depredations, and these savages should be chastised for this terrible foray:

Fort Dodge, Iowa April 13, 1857
To His Excellency,
JAMES W. GRIMES,
Governor of the State of Iowa

Sir: Being called upon by the frontier settlers for aid in checking the horrible outrages committing upon the citizens living on the Little Sioux River, in Clay county, in the Spirit Lake Settlements, and in Emmitt County, by the Sioux Indians, by authority you vested in me, I raised and organized three companies of 25 men each, which were as we proceeded increased to over 30 men each. We took up our line of march on the 25th of March and proceeded up the west branch of the Des Moines river to intercept the savages, who, the report said, were about to sweep all the settlements on the river. By forced marches through snow banks from 15 to 20 feet deep, and swollen streams, we forced our way up to the State line, where we learned the Indians were embodied two or three hundred strong, at Spirit Lake and Big Island groves. Never was harder services rendered by any body of men than by those 110 men under my command. We had to ford streams breast deep every few miles, and at all snow banks or drifts had to shovel roads and draw our wagons through by hand with tug ropes, also the oxen and horses. All were wet all day up to the middle at least, and lay out on the open prairies at night without tents or other covering than a blanket or buffalo robe. About 80 miles up we met those who had escaped the massacre at Springfield, composed of three men unhurt, and one female wounded, and several other women and children, in all numbering 15 or 20 persons. They had escaped in the night, carrying nothing with them but what they had on when they were attacked - had nothing to eat for two days and one night. They were about exhausted and the Indians on their trail pursuing them. Had not our scouts discovered them and reported, there can be no doubt but that they all would have been murdered that night. We found them in a miserable condition, destitute of everything like clothing and food, three of them badly wounded and several of the women without bonnets or shoes. They had nothing on them but what they had the night they fled. The poor women wading breast deep through snow and water and carrying their crying children.

We halted at a small lake that furnished sufficient timber to make fires and warm them - furnished them with provisions and gave them blankets to shield them from the severe weather, and gave them all the relief in our power. Our surgeon dressed the wounds of the wounded, whose wounds were in a bad condition. We encamped there with them that night, posting sentinels and pickets, expecting to be attacked. Next morning we sent them on with scouts to what is known as the Irish settlement to remain until we returned. The settlers above that point having abandoned their homes and embodied themselves at that place where they engaged in building a Block House. We proceeded on our march, throwing out in advance some 30 scouts reconnoitering[93] and examining every point where the enemy might possibly be found-every point of timber, lake and stream was closely

---

[93] make a military observation

examined, and found very fresh traces of the Indians throughout the day. From these tracks and trails they had all taken their course for Spirit Lake, or in that direction. By forced marches we reached the State line, near Springfield, and encamped about sundown on the margin of a grove-detailed 60 men, armed with rifles and six-shooters, with orders to cook their suppers and supply themselves with cold rations, each company their own, and be ready to march all night, in two divisions of 30 men each, and surprise the Indians before daylight next morning. Furnished with guides, as the information we had just received was that the Indians were embodied at or near the trading house of a half-breed, by the name of Caboo.

We proceeded with great hopes of overtaking and giving a good account of them; but to our great mortification[94], we found they had all fled upon the approach of fifty regulars from Ft. Ridgely. Woods & Caboo, traders, gave them the information that the troops were coming, and whose movements they sent their runners out to watch. Had they not sent to Ridgely for troops we would most certainly have overtaken them.

The conduct of the troops from Fort Ridgely is hard to be accounted for. On Thursday, the 27th of March, the Indians attacked Springfield and neighborhood. The citizens defended themselves as well as they could. The battle and pillaging[95] lasted until nightfall, when the Indians withdrew: On Friday in the afternoon the troops from Ridgely arrived all well mounted on mules. Those troops lay at Springfield all day Saturday and assisted in burying some of the dead. Their officers counseled with the half-breed Caboo, who was the only one left unharmed, and known to be acting with and identified with the Indians, and whose squaw (he is married to a squaw,) was, at the time, wearing the shawl of Mrs. Church, with other articles taken from the citizens. Said officers lay over from Friday evening till Sunday morning without

---

[94] great embarrassment and shame.
[95] steal (something) using violence, especially in wartime.

pursuing or making any effort to overtake the Indians, who, they must have known, had taken off four white women as prisoners.

On Sunday morning he set out on their trail, and followed them half the day, finding their camp fires and overtaking three or four straggling squaws, let them go-and finding all kinds of goods thrown and strewed along their trail to lighten their loads and expedite their flight. When he could not have been more than half a day's march from them, he stopped and returned the same evening, (Sunday,) to Springfield. When he ordered the men to return, they expressed a wish to follow on, and said they would put up with half rations if he would allow it. His reply was he had no orders to follow them.

On Monday he set out to Spirit Lake to bury the dead, etc., he went to the first house, that of Mr. Naples, found one dead body, buried it, and returned to Springfield. 'Tis certain troops, or rather such officers, will afford no protection to our frontier settlers. Such men are not fit to protect our frontiers. Think of his conduct; his men all well mounted, turning back when he was not half a days march off them; they loaded down with plunder, and horses and mules, and carrying off with them four respectable women as prisoners. The Indians were known to have some 25 or 30 head of horses and 8 or 10 mules, taken from the settlers. These Indians commenced low down on Little Sioux River, near the S. W. corner of Buena Vista county, and proceeded to break up and destroy all the settlements of that county, Clay, Dickinson and Emmitt Counties; then intended coming down the west branch as far as they dare.

Throughout their whole course they have completely demolished every settlement, killed all the cattle, ravished the women, and most scandalously abused them. They stood over the men with their gun cocked while engaged in their hellish outrages. Along that river they approached, and got into the houses; through professions of friendship and with a rush seized the men and arms, taking the people by surprise and attacking in such a way that one family could not help the other; all attacked simultaneously, robbed them of everything, and left them helpless in the midst of cold weather and deep snows. They did not commence to kill the settlers until they reached Dickinson County. There at Spirit Lake it appears that the settlers had prepared to defend themselves as well as they could, and from all appearances they fought bravely for their families. The settlers at Spirit Lake numbered over forty souls, no one of whom is left to tell the tale[96]. Finding that the troops from Fort Ridgely had not buried the dead, I detailed 25 men to proceed 12 miles to the lake, and reconnoiter[97] that district, and if no Indians were discovered, to inter[98] the dead, as an act of humanity. Guides were procured, and they set out under the command of Captain Johnstone and Lieut. Maxwell, of Company C. They could find no Indians, found their encampment, and a dreadful destruction of property. They performed the sad duty of interring the dead, so far as they could find any. They found and buried 29 bodies, found the skulls of two who were burned in the ruins of a house, which, with the one buried by the troops at Ridgely, made in all 32 dead found at Spirit Lake-9 killed at Springfield, and 12 missing at the Lakes, certainly killed- it is supposed they are lying off at a distance, killed in-attempting to escape-some two or three were found who had been shot in attempting to escape, four of their women taken off as prisoners, and three badly wounded. I may sum up as follows: In all 41 killed: 12 missing, no doubt killed: 3 badly wounded, 2 I fear mortally; 4 women prisoners, besides several men from Boon river and counties east of this, who crossed the Des Moines river, with a view of going to Dickinson county and the Lakes-have never yet been heard from, supposed to have been killed on the way.

From all appearances, the Sioux Indians have determined to wage a war of extermination on our frontiers, as everything goes to show it at every point on the upper Des Moines, Big

---

[96] Actually one survivor – Abbie Gardner
[97] make a military observation
[98] to place (a dead body) in a grave or tomb; bury

Island Grove, Spirit Lake, and all points where we found traces of them. They had left the most threatening signs, stakes set up and painted red, trees barked and painted, representing men pierced with arrows, etc.- At every point they broke up and destroyed all furniture, burnt the houses and killed the cattle-over 100 head of fine cattle were found shot down and untouched in any but knocking off the horns, I suppose to make powder horns; their whole course goes to show that they intend to break up and stop the settlement of the north and north-west country.

Too much praise cannot be bestowed on the men I have under my command on this occasion Officers and men, without exception, have done their duty; they endured the greatest privations and fatigue without a murmur, for seventeen days they pressed forward on their march waded rivers and creeks breast deep, and tugged wagons through snow banks, sleeping on the prairies frequently in their wet clothes, expecting every mile after reaching 30 miles, to meet the Indians, and their threat was at Sioux river, that they would sweep the Des Moines river settlements. Our men suffered very much, owing to the severe change and snow storms. We have 14 men very badly frozen and two lost. Capt. Johnson of Webster city, and Mr. Burkholder of this place; both frozen to death in a snow storm-they were separated in returning from the Lake. From the state of the men who succeeded in getting back to camp, both of these men must be dead: every search has been made for them, but no discovery as yet. So severe was the weather that those who were picked up and did get in, were so much frozen and exhausted that they were crawling on their hands and knees when found and three or four of them had lost their minds becoming perfectly deranged for a time, knew no one.

As near as I could ascertain, the Indian force was from 150 to 200 warriors, judging from their encampments, etc, the number of Indians must be from 15 to 20 killed and wounded. From the number seen to fall killed, and judging from the bloody cloths and clots of blood in their encampments, the struggle at the Lakes must have been severe, particularly the one at the house of Esq. Mattock. Eleven dead bodies were found at this house, together with several broken guns-they appear to have fought hand to hand.

I have to inform your Excellency that we have driven out of the north part of the State every Indian, and can say that at present there are no Sioux in the State, unless it be in that part near the mouth of Big Sioux. The whole body have fled in the direction of the Missouri: crossing the Big Sioux. I shall not be surprised to hear of an attack on Sioux City. I am satisfied that the greater number of these Indians were from the Missouri, as they were strangers to the settlers where they appeared, and a portion of them were half-breeds. Never in the history of our country has such outrageous acts been committed on any people. We have no account of Indians committing such outrages on females as they have done- no doubt committed by the half-breeds.

It is to be feared that they will repeat their depredations, if some measure are not taken to prevent it. They are well armed and well supplied with ammunition. They took 17 kegs of powder with buckshot and lead from Woods at Springfield, burnt his store, and killed him, etc. We have a host of destitute and wounded persons thrown upon us to provide for both from Little Sioux River, and the Upper Des Moines River as well as our own frozen and disabled men. I forward this hasty and somewhat confused report; will give another soon, more in detail. I instructed Capt. Richards, Mr. Morrison and others, to forward to you the affidavits, &c, to apprize you of our marching to relieve the frontiers, &c.

Very respectfully yours,   Wm. Williams

More Indian Hostilities!

Warning that the Indians are preparing for another massacre in Northwest Iowa – "The Valley Whig" - Nov. 15, 1858.

More Depredations[99] on the Frontier!

We learn that there are unmistakable indications of a general hostile feeling amongst the Indians along our northern frontier, and that the impunity which has hitherto attended their outrages inspires them with confidence in their attempted repetition.

A special messenger has arrived from Spirit Lake with dispatches for Gov. Lowe, representing that the Indians are collecting in larger numbers than ever upon our frontiers. The tone and bearing of these Indians is bold, insolent and threatening, and they have already committed numerous depredations upon the property of the white settlers in the vicinity of Spirit Lake. The horses and cattle of the citizens disappear mysteriously, and in several instances it has been ascertained that they were stolen by the Indians.

Miss Gardner, one of the captives taken and released in the spring of 1857 is again living at Spirit Lake, and recognizes amongst these Indians some of Inkpaduta's[100] band who were engaged in the butchery of our citizens that winter, and by whom she and others were taken captive. The danger of similar hostilities is regarded as imminent, and settlers are standing on guard day and night and will continue to do so till a military force shall be sent for their relief and protection.

We are happy to learn that they will not be kept in suspense nor disappointed in their hopes of aid from the Governor. Upon the reception of the intelligence that our fellow citizens were again exposed to the peril of the bloody scenes enacted winter before last in the vicinity of Spirit Lake, Gov. Lowe

---

[99] attacks or plundering
[100] Sub-Chief to Black Hawk

promptly issued orders to Captain Martin of the Frontier Guards, requiring him to march with his company of about fifty men with all possible dispatch to the scene of danger. Captain Martin is directed to take no offensive measures of hostility against the Indians unless such measures are absolutely necessary for the protection and safety of the settlers. He is required, however, to notify all the Indians in that vicinity, whether hostile or friendly to leave the State, and in case of their neglect or refusal to leave, he is instructed to drive them out of the State at all hazards; and he is especially enjoined[101] to make every possible effort to capture Inkpaduta and as many of his tribe as can be identified as implicated in the massacres of the spring of 1857, in order that they may be dealt with according to law.

By a law enacted last winter it is made the duty of the Governor to afford protection to the frontier settlements against the incursions of hostile Indians until adequate protection should be provided by the Federal Government. Notwithstanding the fact that scores of our citizens were massacred by the Indians and that their surviving friends and relatives petitioned the President for redress and protection, the Federal Government has never raised a finger toward affording either. So the law of last winter still remains in force, and the duty of the Federal Government is devolved upon the Governor of the State of Iowa.

It is very generally believed by those who have the best facilities for knowing, that there is a malignant and settled hostility in the breasts of Inkpaduta and the Indians who are under his control, against the whites, and that they are determined to wreak their hostility on our exposed frontier settlements. We understand that Gov. Lowe has made the most urgent representations of the perilous condition of these settlements to the Executive at Washington, and we would unite with him, on behalf of our people, in demanding the prompt interposition of the General Government for the protection of our frontier.

---

[101] Urged or instructed to do

FIRST SETTLERS OF VAN BUREN COUNTY

These settler descriptions were written by A.W. HARLAN and published in "The Daily Gate City" from Feb – Sept 1870.

James Alfrey and his wife - the two should be inseparable, having been husband and wife for more than fifty years. They are both of dark complexion and were from off the Big Sandy, in Kentucky, to Missouri, and from Missouri on to the Des Moines. There is nothing peculiar about either of them. They have raised thirteen children of their own. They had some ten or eleven children when they came here, and that is now going on thirty-five years. They have also had the care of several of their grand children. Mrs. Alfrey is still seemingly as smart as most women of only forty years of age, though she is sixty. Mr. Alfrey is now going on seventy-two years of age, and although somewhat nervous, his eye sight is pretty good. I called on him a few days ago and found him making an ax handle; went with him into his house and found his wife weaving carpet on a neat loom made by Mr. Alfrey himself only last year. Mr. Alfrey, like most men that were raised in that part of Kentucky, was considerably dissipated for more than twenty years, but certainly deserves all the more credit for having reformed most effectually, and has now been a sober man for near twenty years; and with his reform from drunkenness he became a professor of religion of a sect (though not a sect) known as Campbellites[102], who take the Bible for their guide. His wife is also a member of the same church. The two old people together, both having an abiding faith in their religion, are cheerfully awaiting the call to pass through the valley of the shadow of death, fearing no evil.

They let the world wag as it will,
Pray to God and do their duty still.

---

[102] Follower of Thomas Campbell – Disciples of Christ originated from him.

Mrs. Alfrey has always enjoyed remarkable health. The old gentleman is now enjoying much better health than he has done for some years, and thinks that it is much owing to his using water from the oil well which is near him.

1836-37 ledger from Bedell's store in Sweet Home, MO

William Nelson, better known as Old Baggy, was rather a small man of light complexion, raised in North Carolina, and obtained his nickname in the following manner: There was a merchant in that section of the country whose name was Baggy; he had been to Raleigh, North Carolina, for goods and bought for himself one palm leaf hat, the first that was ever seen in that section of country, and wore it some months as a curiosity. On his next trip to Raleigh, N.C. , to replenish his stock of goods, he brought back for sale some half dozen palm leaf hats. William Nelson, then a boy of sixteen, bought the first one that he sold and wore it the next day to a Baptist Association. Some of the boys pretended to think that he was Mr. Baggy the merchant. A small fight ensued; hence then nickname Baggy stuck to him as long as he lived. He died in Missouri some eight or ten years ago, at the age of about sixty-six. The nickname having stuck to him about fifty years so tenaciously that but few persons knew that his name was William Nelson.

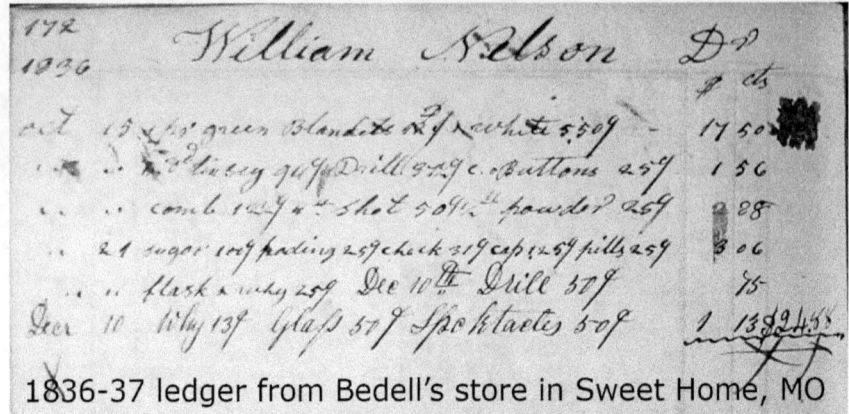
1836-37 ledger from Bedell's store in Sweet Home, MO

Richard M. Jones, was also a North Carolinian; a tolerable fair specimen of a man rather above the medium height. He was a man of tolerable abilities, and was at one time Sheriff of some county in Missouri, Ralls, I believe, and in the discharge of his official duties, it was alleged by his political enemies that on several occasions, he stayed all night at a tavern kept by a widow woman, when if he had rode long enough, that he might have got home; hence, his name Tricky Dick, that always adhered to him. The last I knew of him he was living in Jefferson County, Iowa.

Abel Galland

Abel Galland was a man about six feet high, of doubtful complexion, and had one of the smallest specimens of femininity for a wife that had ever been seen in this section of country. She bore a strong resemblance to a large Dutch doll, yet in some respects was a fit companion for him, for they were both in favor of doing every thing after the most primitive style - save and excepting their religious views that were always of the most recent fanaticism.

I once heard him say that he had changed his religious views some seven or eight times, and after that time I knew him to join the Mormons proper. He followed them as far as Council Bluffs. When they migrated his faith faltered and he retreated a few miles, and was the first settler at what was used to be called Galland's Grove. There he attached himself to the Strangers and migrated to Beaver Island, in Lake Michigan. Here a small schism occurred, and he went with the first party of Mormons to Grand Traverse, Michigan.

Now, I should say if the Lord has any design in making men he must have made Abel Galland for a pioneer. He served in the regular army of the United States five years in his youth, in Illinois and Missouri. He could not bear to live in the settlements, and firmly believed the good country was always a few miles further ahead. He would sell his improvements and move again. His wants were few. With an acre or two of corn, his rifle could supply him with meat. Then he was an excellent bee hunter, and with hominy, milk, venison, and honey, why should a mortal want anything more here below - unless it was a suit of buckskin, and that he always had of the best.

He died some ten or twelve years ago somewhere near Beaver Island', in the northeast end of Michigan lake. At last he has found a resting place. Whether he ever found the good place, we have no report from him.

1836-37 ledger from Bedell's store in Sweet Home, MO

William Jordan was a Virginian by birth. He came west when quite a young man, engaged in mining about Galena, Ill., and afterwards engaged as a hand among the fur traders, before he settled on the Des Moines. He was, perhaps, a light-complexioned man, something less than six feet in height, of stout build and remarkably hairy all over, so much so that the Indians called him the hairy Breasted warrior; and to take him up one side and down the other, he was a pretty good kind of a man. But he, also, became a Mormon, and the last I ever saw of him, he was living: on the Boyer, some distance back and above from Council Bluffs, in Iowa.

Perhaps it would be well here to say that this William Jordan was not any way related to the other Jordan that, figured, also, as an Indian trader, and settled along the Des Moines, River at an early day.

John Petri, I believe, is still living on his original claim, one of the old respectable citizens of Van Buren County, but, like many others, he wanted to see the great plains and the Rocky Mountains, so he, too, went to California for a summer frolic, so when he returned he could say that he had "seen the elephant," also. He then went to work quietly. I learn, on further inquiry, that he has been dead several years.

1836-37 ledger from Bedell's store in Sweet Home, MO

A. W. Harlan In order to make other sketches plain and easily comprehended, I am necessarily compelled to give a short account of my own occupation and whereabouts.

I left the Beaver Des Moines with the number of settlers that I have already named in Van Buren County, and started for Galena or Dubuque. When I Reached Camp Des Moines, the quarters then being constructed by Government under the Superintendency of Lieut. G.H. Crossman, of the 6th U S infantry, and or the reception of three companies of the 1st U.S. dragoons. The place has for many years and is now known as Montrose, in Lee County, Iowa.

I reached that place about the 20th of September, 1834. The wind blew so hard for 48 hours that the ferry could not cross the river, the boat being at that time but a small frail affair. The Lieutenant was in want of hands, and persuaded me to turn out my horse with some other horses and engage at work on the garrison; with the rare privilege, voluntarily offered to me, of lodging with the quartermaster's clerk, a Mr. Tebiman, a Prussian by birth. But I was to board with Capt. James White, who at that time boarded most of the hands that were at work at the quarters. Although I was not a mechanic of any kind, I picked up a jack plane and made a hand with others. I worked for some six or seven weeks and done some of that rough framing of the first stables. At this place I made many acquaintances, some of whom I have never seen since; but amongst them there was Hazen Sweasey and William Bratten, that like myself, were amongst the first settlers of the valley of the Des Moines.

On the following Sabbath I went out to hunt up my horse and made the acquaintance of **Giles Sullivan**, then living near two miles below on the place known as the Burtis place.

This Giles Sullivan proved my evil genius, and if I could make some other things plain for my own credit and that of other persons, I should like to draw this narrative to a close.

However, let me proceed: Sullivan learned from me the price of my horse, and the following week, perhaps, some strangers, looking at the country, came along. One of their horses got kicked and lamed so he could not travel, and Sullivan swapped off my horse to them and got one of his own, and came to me offering me all the money he had, some $80. I told him that would not do, so he borrowed some more money and give to me, with his note for fifteen dollars, inviting me to come down and see him whenever I could make it convenient, saying he was poor but liberal. I made a good many enquiries about him, and here I must say he had many warm friends and about as many bitter enemies.

I looked at the surrounding country, calculated its future importance as a commercial point, concluded to locate on the bluff a little above Keokuk and follow boating or lighting on the rapids. The work on the garrison was finished, the boating season was almost over; I had some money, about ninety dollars; I knew some persons would sell whisky to the soldiers the coming winter, and argued with my conscience as others have done. Sullivan offered to rent me one of his cabins. (The evil genius prevailed.) I went to St. Louis and invested about my bottom dollar in liquors, brought them on and opened out a small grog shop about the first of December, 1834. My compunctions[103] of conscience were not quieted.

---

[103] feeling of guilt that follows doing something bad

My regrets soon followed. One morning I went up to the garrison and found several of my best customers tied up by their thumbs with their hands raised above their heads, as punishment for getting drunk on my whisky.

My trouble did not end here. A few days afterwards Sullivan and myself had been up to the settlers to grind our axes. In passing down, near Col. Kearney's quarters, he hailed me, made a few inquiries, and was answered promptly. He then made some threats. Sullivan told me to talk up to him. I did talk up, as it ultimately proved to my sorrow.

And to make the matter worse, Sullivan talked up some also. He told the Colonel that his bay was stacked rather too close to his quarters. Just at that time we had the best of the quarrel. But Colonel Kearney was an old soldier that knew how to deal with much older rascals than we were.

About one month previous to this time the laws of Michigan had been extended over us by proclamation; that was all. On the arrival of Col. Kearney with his three companies of dragoons, he reigned supreme in all the country north of the State of Missouri and west of the Mississippi.

Within a day or two I received a visit from Captain Brown and Lieut. Berquinn. Capt. Brown bought a half gallon of whisky of me, drank some, his dignity thawed somewhat, he became sociable, inquired of Sullivan about that little quarrel. Sullivan made it a little worse than it really was. I thought I could see through their sociability, but Sullivan, though an old coon, did not. After a time Berquinn took me to one side, gave me the Col's. Compliments and politely informed me that Colonel Kearney would expect me, within a few days, to leave that location.

I had some time for cool reflection. I sold my stock of liquor to Ezra Overhall, and I immigrated to the Des Moines. The following week Col. Kearney sent down a small detachment and poured out the balance of the whisky. Although I have always been a sober man, whisky has been the bane[104] of my life, because others got drunk. Whisky got me into several small scrapes in the Wabash country, in Indiana. Then it was the cause of a much more serious scrape, near Independence, Missouri, and yet some others afterwards on the Des Moines. So, no wonder that I have adopted the Indian theory that "Whisky is the devil."

1836-37 ledger from Bedell's store in Sweet Home, MO

---

[104] cause of great distress

Captain James White must have been one of the first settlers in Hancock County, Illinois; however, I found him, in September, 1834, where the town of Montrose now stands. He must have went there as early as 1833, for he had fenced and planted quite a large field in corn before Lieut. Crossman selected his place on which to build Camp Des Moines.

He was rather a heavy-set man; about five feet ten inches in height, had a loud, coarse voice, and from the run of his conversation must have been amongst the first keel boat captains on the Western waters. He still owned, in 1834, the keel boat "Bronthes." His keel boat and his big stone house just across the river were frequent topics of conversation with him; and when anything had to be done his favorite by-word was "Go it, or bust, by God!" I presume that I have heard him utter that single sentence twenty times a day.

Then I remember that Captain White had a lot of hogs, some forty in number, fifteen or twenty of which were very nice ones, be sides some five or six were running around that Sullivan claimed.

On one occasion Sullivan and myself were invited to dine with a soldiers' mess. They complained of their fat pork. Sullivan inquired if they did not know how to get fresh Pork. One Sheldon replied that hogs would occasionally squeal. Sullivan told him that he had a charm by which he could make a hog roll over in its bed without ever squealing, and lay still to be stuck. The dragoon was anxious to learn. Sullivan then communicated the secret, on condition that his shoats[105] were to be spared. Fresh pork was plenty with some messes until Captain White's hogs were all gone, as well Sullivan's shouts.

I have never tried the charm, and even if I had done so, and knew that it would work, I would not communicate the secret for fear that perhaps I might possibly lose some shoats, as Sullivan did in this case.

Captain White did considerable business. He could not keep his own accounts, and in addition many of those with whom he dealt were much more ignorant than the Captain.

The result was frequent disputes; occasionally the lie was given, and some times a knock-down followed. Sometimes the old Captain got the worst of a fight, but then he did not seem to take it to heart seriously.

Such a scene had happened one morning. I was fixing up some additional shelving in the Settler's Store. White came in, and shortly, after, the man with whom he had the difficulty. Some one referred to the fight. The man said "that old Jim White was the biggest liar that he ever knew." White replied that "he was the most truthful man in the house." The other man, of course, after having made such an accusation would dispute the point. The Captain would make a slight change in the proposition; he would offer to bet a bottle of wine that there was more truth in him than any man in the house. The bet was generally taken. The Captain would then get his opponent to admit that at the birth of each and every person, they respectively contained an equal amount of truth. The old Captain would then enquire of all present if any of us had ever known him to tell the truth when a lie would possibly do. The testimony was always clear that the truth was pretty much all still left in the Captain. About this stage of the joke the stranger would begin to see the point and fork over. I

---

[105] young, weaned pigs or piglets

testified for him once, and helped drink the wine on two occasions; on both of which future friendship was pledged.

I had considerable dealings with Captain James White, and found him always truthful and honest, but I kept a plain account. Some of his-grandchildren are still on the waters, and are respectable and refined.

It is the times that develop men of a certain cast to suit the times, as the revolution of France developed Napoleon the First; as the late rebellion developed Grant.

The old Captain's stone house has had many different occupants since he passed off the stage of action.

About the 20th of December, 1834, I returned to the Des Moines. Samuel C. Reid had moved to his place just above what is now known as Reid's creek. John Slaughter, a single man, made his home with him. Jeff Jordan was living on the opposite side of the river, though a little higher up. James Sanders was living in the next Bottom above; that is to say, about one and a half miles below, where Bentonsport is now situated, on the opposite side of the river. Giles O'Sullivan, Henry Plummer, O.P. Thomas and A.W. Harlan struck camp just above where the business part of Bentonsport is now situated. Sullivan having previously made a claim, we cut logs, hauled them and erected a double log house a little above where the mills now, stand, close on the bank of the river. O.P. Thomas was the stone mason that built the fire place. The rest of us made boards, put on the roof, chinked the cracks and daubed them with mud, cold as the weather was, and was under shelter Christmas day, 1834. Sullivan's wife and family reached, here, I believe, New Year's day, 1835 and within a day or two I purchased a claim of old Capt. Forquerean, about a mile above, and from that date should be considered one of the settlers, although I did not commence keeping batch[106] until about the first of February, 1835, and for about four months was the frontier settler; that is, the highest up the river. James Powel moved in on the opposite

---

[106] Living as a bachelor

side of the river, about two miles above, about the first of May, 1835. Dr Isaac McCarty moved in next above him about the last days of May, 1835, nearly opposite the mouth of Rock Creek.

Ansons – Frank, George & Henry

About the first week in June, 1835, Frank Anson, George Anson, Henry Anson and Seth Pratt, came and settled or at least cleared a small patch and planted some corn, still above where McCarty lived. That is nearly opposite the mouth of Rock Creek, one of the last places that should be named.

There were several trading houses still higher up the river, but I have now mentioned the last corn patch planted in the spring of 1835.

Peter Gillis settled, in the fall of 1835, at the rapids on the south side of the Des Moines, nearly opposite where Kinnersly's mill now stands.

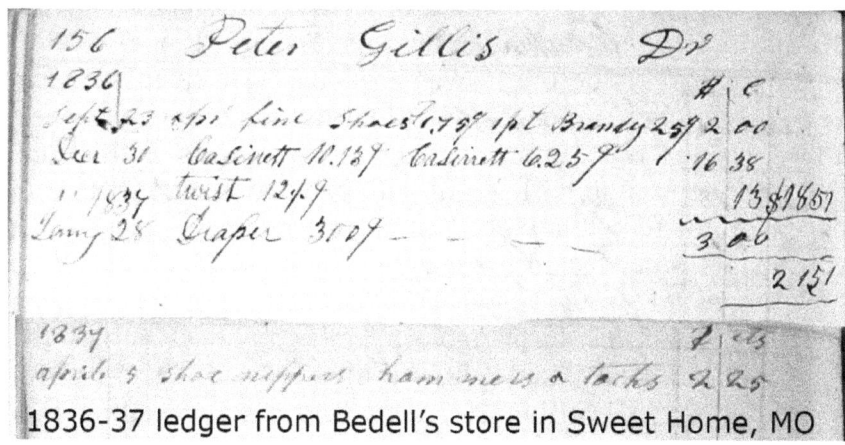

1836-37 ledger from Bedell's store in Sweet Home, MO

Elijah Purdom Sr. arrived and settled a little above where Keosauqua is at this date. He had a large family, and in addition thereto, there was three young men by the name of Vannoy come along with them who made claims. There was also one John Tilvers, an old bachelor, who made the first claim where Keosauqua is now situated.

David A. Ely and John Goodwin also come in and settled a little further up the bottom, having previously made their claims. The foregoing names include all the actual settlers up to January, 1st, 1836, although there were many claims made still higher up the river. True there were several others moved in lower down the river.

A few persons had made claims out on the edge of the prairie, but up to January, 1836, no prairie breaking had been done.

The future denizens of this prairie country may wonder at the fact of all the first settlements being made on the river amongst heavy timber, but they will please bear in mind that there was few of us able to own a prairie team, while with our axes we could clear a small patch.

Giles Sullivan was a character here in an early day. I believe he was born in Kentucky and raised about St. Louis, Mo.

He was among the first settlers in almost every county on the Mississippi River from St. Louis up to Clark, though he left Clark some years before it, was organized. He lived near two years about two miles below Montrose, and in December, 1834, was the first settler at Bentonsport, and up to this time had only been plain Giles Sullivan, but one evening while in camp he got to blarneying[107] me a little, or, in other words, soft soaping me. I paid back in the same coin, eulogized the O'Sullivans of Ireland, told him he had as good as been cheated out of his birth-right, by taking the O out of the family name. That joke took with him. I learned him how to insert the O in spelling his name and always calling him O'Sullivan. This was the christening. From that time he used the O. I might here assert that he is not the only man that I re-named or dubbed. At the time he came here he was about thirty seven years of age, about five feet eight inches in height, and weighed 140 pounds; stood erect, in short, built up for endurance. His Indian name was Muscoet-ipaw, signifying red-whiskers.

---

[107] using charm and pleasant flattery to persuade

He had many good traits, and a good many traits that were not so very good. He always had his warm friends and bitter enemies; pretty equally divided in opinion. It seemed that he could not live without doing kind acts; and then, on the other hand, he could not enjoy life without an occasional quarrel. He delighted in seeing other men fight, and did not object to taking a hand occasionally himself. He had a great deal to say about dueling, encouraged the practice, and would, upon a pinch, do a little shooting himself. He was quite poor when he came here, and necessity compelled him to be rather sharp on small trades. Francis Church and Charles O. Sanford bought part of his claim in 1835 and laid out the town of Bentonsport in the spring of 1836. From that time for about two years Giles O'Sullivan prospered, so much so that he built him a new house and had left at one time three thousand dollars, all in silver. Then he bought part of his town back again, commenced making a farm out back from the town, and soon got into difficulties.

The early court records have a good deal to say about O'Sullivan and Ross, and Ross' "nigger," for be it known that there was an attempt made to establish slavery here, in spite of law and the people, but it was crushed out after almost ruining O'Sullivan and Ross.

Giles O'Sullivan then emigrated to Texas and commenced the world anew, after he was more than forty years of age, and after having some more ups and downs, it is said that he was thrown from his horse and killed.

Giles O'Sullivan at this time had his second wife, one amongst the good women of the world. She was the daughter of Thos. Willis, one among the early settlers of Hancock County, Illinois. He refused to let O'Sullivan have his daughter. She was not yet eighteen years old. License was necessary. O'Sullivan went to the Clerk's office, then at Monticello. The clerk flatly refused the license, but his office was not well arranged; his papers were all in an open box; O'Sullivan quietly took up a fire shovel full of coals and pointed to the papers, and peremptorily ordered him to issue the license. He knew the man he had to deal with; the license was issued without further objections.

Winnena Sullivan was perhaps about as good a wife as any man was ever blessed with. She was a stout, robust woman, with black hair, and, a large liquid black eye that has seldom been surpassed. Her education was limited, but her knowledge of house keeping and economy was hard to beat. Her disposition was almost angelic. She would often chide[108] her husband mildly, and when he did not do right, in paying for work to different young men that he hired, she would sometimes make amends to them by making a shirt or two for them without charge, and in this way she had no enemies. I would not say that she has suffered much from hardships. Her life has been truly a romantic one. She left Bentonsport, Iowa, about 1839, and went with her husband to Texas and on to the frontier. Since that time she has went two or three trips from Iowa to the Green River country, in Kentucky, in settling up her father's estate. And also two trips to Texas and back in adjusting her husband's business. She also went to California, and remained about a year, and returned Kentucky, and again went to California, and from thence to British Columbia, remained about a year, and then returned to Missouri, and was, in December, 1861, residing about two miles north of Lancaster, in Schuyler County, Missouri with her third husband, whose name is Newman. She still enjoyed tolerable health, although she said the breaking out of the war affected her memory. This was only two days after the first battle of Lancaster, that I paid her a visit at the risk of my life, and came near losing that, being waylaid by some bushwhackers.

Her children have all died. Her only son concluded to leave Texas about 1859; turned all of his property into cash and cattle and started for Iowa, and was robbed and murdered by his hired hand. Such is life on the frontier.

---

[108] To scold or rebuke

Samuel C. Reid[109] was among the first Justices of the Peace made after the organization of Iowa, and may have been commissioned under Wisconsin rule and held over and re-appointed. He was a light complexioned, bony man, near six feet in height, and, I think, the best description of his phiz[110] that could be given, would be to borrow a description of him by Morton Nelson, who was himself a remarkably homely boy of sixteen, and the son of a shoe-maker. They had a falling out. Reid told him of his ugly looks. He retorted by telling Reid that the skin of his face looked like it had been drawn on, by a pair of shoe-makers' pinchers, and that his mouth was cut the wrong way of the leather.

Samuel C. Reid, Esq., had many faults. They were too numerous to mention. He had many redeeming qualities, and I shall try to recapitulate some of them. He was a tolerable judge of law; he kept a pretty fair looking docket; he never interfered in his neighbors' difficulties until they got through fighting and settled the doctor bills. Then he always urged them to appeal to law, so as to give lawyers and judges a chance for a livelihood. He never interfered in a quarrel; thought it best to let it come to a head the usual way. He did not believe in punishing criminals in the State prison as that was expensive. He thought it a better plan to have the lawyers to fleece the rogues out of all their stealings and let the county pay the costs. He believed in providing for his own household, and in so doing prove to the world that he was better than an infidel. His most shining virtue was he had some fear of future punishment and was long known by the nick-name of "Salty Sam."

---

[109] The document shows Reed; Corrected to Reid as used elsewhere
[110] A persons face or expression

CAPT. SHAPLEY P. ROSS

Shapley P. Ross with his family arrived on the ground about the 20th of April, 1835, and settled adjoining Sullivan, above, on the River. He had made his claim in the fall of 1834. Mr. Ross was a rather fine looking man, being something over six feet high, perfectly straight, well muscled of rather dark complexion, mouth rather large for beauty, and weighted near two hundred pounds. He was a cousin to Giles O. Sullivan. They were closely connected in nearly all their transactions, and finally went to Texas together. The last I heard of Ross, he had a sub-agency among the Comanche Indians, and had become wealthy.

Willcock also came in about the first of April, 1835, and settled next below James Sanders, or, in other words, on the bottom on the opposite side of the river, about 1 ½ miles above Bonaparte. He had a large family – I think twelve children. They raised an excellent garden and a small field of corn the first season. Their supply of bacon gave out in July, and the old man had no means of laying in any more, so they tried the experiment of living on garden vegetables, roasting ears, etc. The result was the old people died and four of the children, all in a short time, while yet on the place, and I think one or two of them died after their uncle David Willcock took them back to Palmyra, Missouri. The above is the most fatal of the sickness known on the river.

Nowell – I have forgotten his given name and may have forgotten how to spell his surname – came and settled near the ford on Indian Creek; in the fall of 1835 (I believe there is a Mr. Burner now living on the place.) Mr. Nowell was our first sheriff under the Wisconsin rule, and like all men that had held office, had his enemies as well as friends. But it is only some circumstances of frontier life that I shall relate in connection with his name.

He had a large family, eleven children, I think. He had a parcel of hounds, seven in number. His cabin (he had but one) was sixteen feet square, with a linn[111] puncheon[112] floor, with large cracks between the puncheons. The foundation of his cabin was placed on some chunks so that there was more than a foot of open space between the puncheons and the ground, so that the wind had a fair sweep beneath.

I think it was in February, 1837, the first time that I ever went from near Keosauqua to mill at Waterloo, Missouri. There had been a thaw that made the ground soft four or five inches deep. As for a road it scarcely could be called a road. There was not travel enough to make mud, as at that time from Waterloo through to Indian Creek there was but some five or six cabins in sight. My companion was Henry Plummer. Our grinding was done in the morning, and it was tolerably pleasant until near nine o'clock; but then the wind began to blow from the north-west and the ground began to freeze, and kept on freezing, and the harder the ground froze the harder the wagon pulled until near night. It had then frozen so as to bear up the wagon, and night now came on before we had reached Mr. Nowell's hospitable residence.

He cheerfully admitted us to his fireside – we had some provisions and blankets with us, as was the custom of the country at that time. This made fifteen persons in that one little room, and most of the time several dogs were in also,

---

[111] Wood from a linden or basswood tree
[112] split log with one face smoothed

for by this time it had become so cold that I believe the dogs would have frozen if they had been shut out of the doors.

Mr. Nowell had no beds. I will not say that bed time came at night, but the time did come when all of us sought a horizontal position for repose. Plummer and I spread our blankets before the fire on the open puncheon floor, pulled off our boots, put them under our heads for pillows, and tried to lie still. But as the wind would drive in under the house, it would force its way up through the cracks in the floor wonderfully and cold at that. The dogs, seven in number, were lying around, whining from cold. At last, one of them came and crawled on to me. You may guess I threw him about six feet, slam on the floor.

We revised our bed by putting our three blankets all on the underside, and then lay down again. Directly a dog came and crawled on me. I took that dog and pulled him under my head for a pillow, and held him there, Plummer having set the example – I do assure you a dog makes a pretty good pillow on a cold night. The dogs kept coming. We arranged them in the most convenient and systematic manner and each of us obtained a comfortable nap, however, long before daylight, when Mr. Nowell called up one of his largest boys to make a fire. As I raised my head and took a view of my bed fellow, I thought we formed a pretty compact body of dogs.

Mr. Nowell lived at that place two or three winters without underpinning or banking his house, and then concluded that this country was rather too cold for him. He then moved to the northern part of Texas bordering on Red River, and I did hear that he has become wealthy.

There has been many a soldier in the late rebellion that would have been thankful for such privileges as we had, and your humble servant among that number.

Dr. A. B. Williams.

Abiatha Buck Williams always had rather a bad reputation, Came to Van Buren County, Iowa, before its organization, that is, he settled in Rising Sun, since known as Pittsburg, in 1837.

He was, at that time, about 31 years of age, near six feet in height, of dark complexion, black hair and eyes. His eyes were bright and piercing, and when he became a little excited they shone with a peculiar luster not easily forgotten.

He brought a small stock of goods with him when he first came and for two or three years following sold goods and studied medicine at the same time. He had a wife and several children. His wife died, I think, in 1840.

He was skeptical in his religious views. He could sustain an argument pretty well, and at times became rather sarcastic, and as he became surrounded by Methodist class leaders and circuit riders, all united in giving him a bad reputation.

He had seemingly a natural contempt for politicians. They soon became a numerous class in so scant a population. Many of them had vulnerable points, and Abiatha would occasionally touch them lightly without respect to party. This brought several of them down on him heavily. They gave him a bad reputation.

Then he had another talent, which, had it been properly cultivated, might have rendered him eminent as an artist. I refer to his capacity for making rough sketches with chalk, one of which made A.B. Williams many enemies.

I never saw that drawing; but Williams said he only took a piece of chalk and scratched a little while on the wall; it was the imagination of other people that invested this small amount of chalk with a striking resemblance, to two of the most prominent candidates, for the Territorial Council. Some boy wrote a short sentence beneath the most prominent figure that had a tendency to attach a rather unpleasant nickname to Dr. J.D. Elbert; so Elbert was rather down on Williams, and concurred in giving him a bad reputation.

Abiatha B. Williams commenced the practice of medicine here amongst us where we were all acquainted with him. He had only tolerable success, but he had no diploma at that time. Neither was there at that time a medical board in the Territory, or a medical college that issued diplomas. Then it was reported that Williams said he did not care for a diploma; that it was only a piece of writing on sheep-skin, signed by some old rascal permitting some young rascal to physic poor devils to death with impunity. Therefore doctors generally gave him a bad reputation.

I will give you one more incident. The people of Van Buren County, Iowa are aware that during the two years of 1838 and 1839 we had all the excitement to the locating of the county seat. I shall not give particulars, as it was only interesting to the people of the county. The writer hereof at that time lived at or near Keosauqua, and opposed the location on principle, as he would do again were it to do over. But Pittsburg, where Williams resided, was a candidate, being only about two miles distant from Keosauqua, but on the opposite side of the river. It was a strong competitor and local interests after a time run into personalities. The petitions, the counter-petitions, the legislation, the elections, and the keen wiggling, chicanery[113] and skullduggery[114] ought to form a long chapter, but I leave it all out.

Amongst all the opponents to the location of the county seat at Keosauqua - and there were several of us I think Abiatha B. Williams was the most prominent, and for that reason the proprietors of Keosauqua united in giving him a bad reputation. And just here I will add that I believe that the old records of the Commissioner's Court show who the parties were that gave their bonds for building the public buildings, but there of is nothing on record to show who made them do it.

I have already stated that A.B. Williams was a widower. He went to Nauvoo and married a beautiful girl whose parents were Mormons. Even this natural and laudable act had a tendency to increase his already bad reputation.

A.B. Williams was a plain out-spoken man, and often told entirely too much truth. This trait in any man's character will, I know from, sad experience, give any man a bad reputation. There was some truth in what he said about diplomas, but a diploma as a general thing is a true certificate that a young man has gone through a certain course of studies and attended certain lectures, &c[115], &c. But even diplomas, like bank bills, are sometimes counterfeited.

But worst of all Abiatha B. Williams was poor in worldly goods, and it is long since some poet sang:

> *Dimes and dollars, dollars and dimes,*
> *An empty pocket is the worst of crimes.*

It was about 1843 that A.B. Williams moved to Montrose, and, renting a tavern stand, commenced keeping a public house and still continued the practice of medicine. These were exciting times, as we all know. The public mind was in a perfect furore[116].

---

[113] deception by sophisticated trickery
[114] underhanded or unscrupulous behavior
[115] Type set for etc. or &
[116] Outbreak of public anger or excitement.

A.B. Williams was a man that could talk. He contended for the constitutional privileged of all religious sects - the Mormons not excepted, holding all alike amenable to the laws of the land. This gave him the nick-name of Jack Mormon, which increased his already bad reputation.

The scenes that occurred hereabouts I shall leave to the historian. I am only trying to write a sketch of A.B. Williams. I think that it was in 1845 that there was a little pamphlet published, purporting to have been written by a man whose, name was Bonney, called "The Banditti of the Prairie." This said pamphlet gave Abiatha B. Williams, a very bad reputation. The pamphlet had at the time an extensive circulation. Many of them are still preserved in this vicinity, and they have a tendency to perpetuate his bad reputation. Whether any of the statements in, that pamphlet were true or not, I do not know; but I do know that A.B. Williams had other and quite different business with the Mormon leaders, the particulars of which may rest for the present. The Mormon expulsion soon followed. A.B. Williams moved to Green Bay, Wisconsin, and in 1850 he went to California. He had no desire to call at Salt Lake and see the Mormon leaders, as he would have been likely to have done had the statements in that pamphlet been facts.

Here, as the lawyers say, I might with safety rest the case, but I will ask the reader to follow me through another chapter.

It was within a few months of the same time that Abiatha B. Williams left Montrose, Iowa, that Barent A. Williams, formerly of Greene County, New York, came and settled at Keokuk. I think that it was in 1846 that I bought the first little bill of goods of him. The two men are nearly of the same age, though I think Abiatha is the oldest, a little the tallest, and had an eye that was apt to leave an impression on first sight; and it is him and his fortunes that we shall follow.

The Mexican war ended, the gold excitement for California soon followed; and who is there that has not heard of the boys of 1849? But it was not until the spring of 1850 that Abiatha B. Williams fitted out some two or three teams and several young men from Green Bay, Wisconsin, himself and part of his family going to California with them; and after prospecting and trying his luck in a few places, he became settled at Tollses Diggings for a few months in the Summer of 1851. In November, 1851, he returned home by steamship and remained in New Orleans, until he could get the identical coin that should be made from his gold dust..

Then A.B. Williams and family kept on their way north to Green Bay, Wisconsin; and in 1853 bought up a drove of cattle, and went back to California. Since that time I have had no definite information from him.

He is most likely alive and still "kicking;" for he is one of the men that will not rust as long as he lives.

It is the custom of writers to enumerate a man's good traits of character only after he dies; but presuming that A.B. Williams is still living, I will try to enumerate a portion of his bad traits of character:

He often espoused[117] a quarrel for a friend when it would have been better for his reputation to have left it alone.

He had a larger amount of abusive epithets at his command than any honest man was entitled to.

He had a mind of his own on every subject; a thing that no poor man is entitled to.

Other traits in his character I have heretofore enumerated, and will only give one more at present:

He openly acknowledged that previous to coming to Iowa he had been a class leader in the Methodist Episcopal Church; that he had tried hard to believe in the doctrine, and could not; that he preferred to be known as an infidel to knowing himself to be a hypocrite.

I wish to close this chapter by expressing my doubts whether A.B. Williams was honestly entitled to the unenviable

---

[117] To support a cause

reputation that he acquired, taking the circumstances into consideration.

I was well aware some twenty-four or twenty-five years ago that quite a number of the first settlers of Keokuk either thought or pretended to think that Barent A. Williams and Abiatha B. Williams were one and the same person; but had supposed for years that said impression had ceased to exist. And it was only last Fall, when in conversation with an old settler and one of our active business men, that I learned that he still held the same opinion. Indeed, he could not be convinced to the contrary, which surprised me very much.

And on further enquiry I found the impression to be general. I was also inclined, to suspect that the impression had been kept up by some designing individuals, but shall make no accusations against any person or persons. I will barely presume that Barent A. Williams may, at some time in his life, had some enemies, and they, finding an unenviable reputation already manufactured, have designedly attached that reputation to quite another individual.

I pretend to say that there is no man that is any man at all but will occasionally have an enemy. If he is unsuccessful in business and cannot pay his honest debts, he is stigmatized as a villain; if he is eminently successful in business, and accumulates a fortune; many persons will envy him his prosperity, and slyly insinuate he must have stolen most of his property.

Now, in closing this sketch, I will say, upon the honor of an early settler of Iowa, that if I was ever acquainted with any man that man was Abiatha B. Williams; one among the first settlers of Van Buren County, Iowa. And that I can give two additional and more substantial reasons than any heretofore given that at least ought to be acquainted with him. To any person residing in Keokuk that may still have doubts on this subject, just call on Henry Hefferman on Johnson Street, in your city. He ought to have been acquainted with Abiatha B. Williams, as he was High Sheriff of Van Buren County at the time of the occurrence of several incidents that I have given in the foregoing sketch.

And finally, let me say that Abiatha B. Williams and Barent A. Williams, of Keokuk, are two separate and distinct men. That I have reason to believe that they are not relatives, and that they never were acquaintances, notwithstanding they were both originally from the State of New York.

SETTLEMENT OF DES MOINES VALLEY

These settler descriptions were written by A.W. HARLAN and published in THE DAILY GATE CITY from Feb – Sept 1870.

Wm. Meek, Jr   William Meek, Sr

Wm. Meek, the founder and proprietor of Bonaparte, in Van Buren County, Iowa, came on to the place in July, 1837. His son, Robert Meek, was with him, he having come to Sand Prairie in November, 1836. The old Judge, as Wm. Meek, Sr., was generally termed, was from the State of Michigan; was of medium height, rather heavy set, with a clear blue eye, pleasant countenance, and at all times easy of approach, and at the time he came here, about sixty-four years of age. He purchased the claim of Robert Moffatt, who lived near where Thomas Charlton resides at this date. That includes the possession of the Meek's above the creek. John Moffatt, the father of said Robert Moffatt, was living on the lower side of the creek, occupying the original Courts claim, which included the present town plat of Bonaparte, and extending back up the creek, covering most of the farm at present occupied by Robert Meek. One purchase included both claims. Judge Meek bought those places for the express purpose of building mills and manufactories, he having previously been engaged in milling in Michigan. He immediately began preparations for building a saw and grist mill - putting his mill houses pretty well out into the river, with a wooden lock for the purpose of passing steamboats. He got his mills in operation in the fall of 1838. There is but little, if anything, remaining at present of the first set of mills or lock.

Wm. Meek had his two sons, Robert and William, who were of age, as partners from the beginning. Isaiah and Joseph were boys under age. The name of the firm was Wm. Meek & Sons. It is now Meek & Brothers.

The firm of Wm. Meek & Sons soon after beginning their mills acquired a reputation for industry, energy and prompt payment of all their contracts, and must have paid to laborers the two first years more than twenty thousand dollars. Although not so successful as he anticipated, still it was a success such as few persons seemed to enjoy.

The old Judge, I believe, was not a professor of religion, but encouraged any religion that inculcated morality. He was always active in the support of common schools, and himself one of the most temperate of men. His example in one other respect is worthy of note. He had lost his wife in about 1849. His children were all grown and had families of their own. The old Judge felt lonesome and almost helpless. As he was now about seventy-five years of age, he concluded to get married. Most people would say it was a foolish notion. Let us see. His mills, farms and everything were in successful operation. Most of it was partnership or family property. The old Judge settled with all his children, giving each one their portion, adjusted everything satisfactorily, reserving to himself only a homestead and a certain amount of money already loaned out. Thus it might be said that Judge Meek administered on his own estate previous to getting married. He made a judicious selection of a stout, hearty widow lady, about fifty-five years of age, with a small family. I saw him but once after his second marriage. He thought he had done well in getting married. He said his new wife was a stout woman, and that she took good care of him. He had a kind wife to soothe him in his last days. He died in 1853, aged 80 years.

The foregoing sketch is but an imperfect one, and I hope some one else may give some additional particulars, as the origin and progress of so prosperous a place as Bonaparte should be noted particularly; neither can the real advantages to community be correctly estimated. The quality of woolen goods at present manufactured at Bonaparte are of the best; the amount is also considerable, paying a handsome revenue to Government, and all resulting from the fact that Wm. Meek, Sen., located at that place and persevered to the end.

The old Judge had managed so judiciously, in family matters as well as mills and manufactory, that all of them moved on without any jar or lawing[118], and still they continue to run.

Isham Keith, with quite a large family of both boys and girls, emigrated from McMinn County, State of Tennessee, and arrived on the bank of the Des Moines, near where Bonaparte is situated, on the 9th of May, 1836, and settled out on the ridge at the edge of the prairie, a mile or two north of Bonaparte, he being the first settler in that locality.

He was a man of medium size, with a gray eye and quite a gray head. His gray hair attracted attention, as there were but comparatively few old men amongst us at that time. He was a man of stern integrity, quite intelligent, and as most of us had heard the proverb, "Old men for council, and young men for war," we elected Isham Keith to the Council of the first Territorial Legislature of Iowa. His son Thomas Keith was the first Assessor of Van Buren County.

The old gentleman died about 1845, and his four sons also died not far from the same time. Thomas and Charles died in Oregon. Alexander at Keokuk, Iowa. Jas. Keith died at Napoleon, in Arkansas. His daughters, four in number, are still living.

---

[118] exercising the practice of law

Thomas Blankenship bought James Sanders' claim on the opposite side of the Des Moines from Bonaparte, and moved on in the fall of 1835. He was a man of medium size, and at that time about 53 years of age. There was a large amount of gas and bombast[119] about old Tom as he was called. He had served in the U.S. army and again as a volunteer in Missouri during the Black Hawk war.

In the spring of 1826, the Methodist church sent one of their circuit riders to the Des Moines. Blankenship's house was one of his stopping points. Old Tom was generally full of piety while the preacher was about, and then when he got where there was whisky, he generally got tolerably full of whisky and at such times was full of fun.

During the summer of 1836, there was several young men came along; some of them stopped to work about Bentonsport. Some of them were somewhat green. Old Blankenship could pick out a green one as quick any man that I ever saw, and for the purpose of sport was always their big friend. When he wanted sport he would treat a young fellow, and be sure to treat himself more liberally, then commence admiring the stranger. He could throw himself into more attitudes than any Kentucky horse jockey, pat the stranger on the shoulders, and sometimes elsewhere, and then step back and admire his muscular developments, exclaiming frequently, "ain't he a beauty!" then walk round the young man again saying, "ain't he to my notion," and again, "he is just to my notion." Sometimes it raised a fuss, but that was just to his liking.

He stayed here about two years, sold out and went back to Missouri. In time of our Mexican war, although he must have been over sixty, he managed to go to Mexico as a volunteer, and was killed at the battle of Monterey. He had a daughter, only moderately good looking, but she had the most splendid

---

[119] high-sounding language with little meaning to impress people

voice for singing that I ever heard. Her voice in some places would have been fortune to her.

The following little incident I see I have inadvertently omitted in the proper place, and it is only a little dog story at best.

By some means Giles O'Sullivan had got possession of a stray dog that was good for running wolves. Blankenship took a fancy to that dog, petted him, and coaxed the dog home with him. This proceeding O'Sullivan objected to. Blankenship contended that he had as good a right to the dog as O'Sullivan, and meant to keep him. One evening O'Sullivan took his rifle gun and went for his dog, and had started away with him. Blankenship followed. The result was they changed some two or three shots each by moonlight, each trying to kill. Each charged the other with shooting first, and all for a stray dog. They agreed in one thing, however, that they were both of them tolerable shots by moonlight. O'Sullivan kept the dog.

Charles Gaston was the first occupant of the claim on which Doctor Bailey at present resides. He came in the fall of 1835. There was also another man by the name of Gaston that made a claim near the same time, some miles above where Keosauqua is at present; but I think that it was Charles that kept bach[120] near Vernon. The two Gastons did not claim kin, however. I have not heard of either of them for more than thirty years.

Joseph Perkins came on to his present location in 1836. A Mr. Samuel Maxwell had previously had a claim near the same place. He may have bought out Maxwell. At least Jo. Maxwell is one amongst the old settlers still on hand at this date, and able to answer for himself.

Isaac Reid, I believe, moved in December 1835, however I am not sure of the time, as I did not become acquainted with

---

[120] A bachelor's crib- small modest home.

him until the Fall of 1836, at which time he was already flourishing like a green bay tree. He was of light complexion, near six feet in height, stout build, mouth rather large, indeed rather coarse all over; he held his head erect, or, as it was often said, he had his eye cocked for the ten o'clock sun, and but seldom looked low enough to discover the beauties of the setting sun.

He was the original proprietor of the once famous town of Lexington, on the river Des Moines, about one mile above where the present town of Bonaparte is situated. During 1837 he sold several lots to individuals, and also joint interests to some others, and for a year or eighteen months considered himself wealthy, and I do not think that he would have taken ten thousand dollars for his possessions.

I also heard him say, on another occasion, that he was sure that in less than five years his town would be more populous than Lexington, in Kentucky. During 1837-8 I had the mail contract, and made Lexington a stopping point one night every week, consequently had excellent opportunities for observation.

I have old Ike Reid still in my eye, as he used to walk out with some stranger, with his cane in hand, after having exhibited his town plat in the house. He would commence marking on the ground with his cane, and if he could find dust or sand, he would soon make a complete plat of Lexington, with its several squares, school houses, and places for churches of different denominations.

He had in his mind's eye a most emphatic vision of the future greatness of his town. I once had the temerity[121] to intimate to him that he might possibly be a little over sighted. I soon learned that any man had better strike him with a club than to doubt the future greatness of Lexington.

He looked on that as a fixed fact, but had no objection to other little places prospering. That Farmington might grow to

---

[121] excessive confidence or boldness, audacity

be a considerable village he went to Farmington in the spring of 1835, just after a big rain, to invest some of his surplus capital in a few lots.

Now in an early day there was some places a little wet in the spring. Reid called on Henry Bateman, the then proprietor, was shown round very politely, and was urged to buy a lot or two on Front street. He finally selected some lots back a considerable distance, where at that time the water was about six inches deep. Mr. Bateman enquired why he chose those lots, and Reid replied that he wanted a location to establish a ferry. There was no trade made that day between those two town proprietors. Not far from the same time Isaac Reid came in control, with Giles O'Sullivan, the proprietor resident of Bentonsport. In eulogizing their respective town sites Isaac was decidedly first best. They then locked horns and gave the crowd a display of pugilistical[122] science interspersed at intervals with ground and lofty tumbling, in which Isaac came out second best only.

The years 1837 and 1838 were glorious years with Isaac Reid. In 1840 Bonaparte began to grow a little. Isaac began to doubt, but still, as he said himself, Isaac kept a stiff upper lip.

In 1842 and 1843 Lexington began to grow smaller by degrees and beautifully less, but the corn field and potatoe patches grew larger, just in the same proportion. In 1850 the once famous city of Lexington had become a corn field, and has now remained so for almost twenty years.

Perhaps it would be well to bear in mind at that time, when a lot of 100 by 150 feet was supposed by some to be worth from $100 to $500, here on the Des Moines, that more than half of the States of Illinois and Missouri had been surveyed and offered for sale, and at that time the government title could be had at one dollar and twenty-five cents per acre, without any restriction as to the amount a man might buy.

---

[122] Related to fist fighting

Isaac Bird was a candidate for Representative in the first Legislature of the Territory of Iowa. Though unsuccessful, some of his speeches were rare specimens of oratory. He was a public spirited man, and liberal when he had means. The last time that I ever saw him was in 1846, and he must have died when I was in California, in 1850 or 1851, and at the time of his death I must have been over fifty years of age. Several members of his family have since died, and the remaining portion have all went to California.

William Fallis was one of the first merchants of the town of Lexington. He was originally from Virginia, but had made a great many moves in his time, and at every move he got rather poorer. His wife was always willing to move with him, and believed that the good place was still ahead. On one occasion she said she believed there was some place where flitters[123] growed on trees and dropped off into a pond of molasses, and that she was willing to keep moving on until they found that place. They remained here but a short time and moved to Texas, but I have never heard whether they ever found the place where flitters growed on trees or not.

James Blankenship came on to the Des Moines with his uncle, Thomas Blankenship. He was a tolerable good looking light complected young man, of something more than medium size. He was, as he said, a kind of rough carpenter, could saw wood and burn coal. He was remarkably fond of a good song, and could do some singing himself. He was a remarkable mimic, loved a good joke, but unfortunately he loved bad whisky.

There was a time in Bentonsport, when a large crowd had collected and they got up a grand display of fisticuffs and other gymnastic exercises. After the ball had fairly opened Jim rolled up his sleeves and exclaimed that he was a little the prettiest child his mother ever raised, and pitched in. He soon ran against one Bill Helm that soon battered his

---

[123] bread cooked similar to pancakes

physiognomy[124] so that on the next day he was not considered so handsome.

The foregoing amusing incident occurred in the spring of 1837, and about the same time there arrived from Massachusetts a little freckled face lawyer, whose name was Buckland. He wanted a case of law bad, so he managed to get him bound over to appear at court, hoping to get a fee in some way or on some side, and he did not care which.

James Blankenship was bound over for rioting, appeared, and, strange to say, the Grand Jury found a bill of indictment, and it was not very strange either. That Grand Jury was a set of good looking old fogies. Most of them had been Justices of the Peace in other States, and had not learned to appreciate our sources of amusement in the Territory of Iowa. The case was tried at the first term of court held by Chief Justice Charles Mason, at Keosauqua, Van Buren County, Iowa. The Petit Jury was empanelled[125] and sworn; the prosecuting attorney read a long rigmarole[126], in which the words "malice prepence[127]," and "contrary to the peace and dignity of the Territory of Iowa," occurred several times, and James Blankenship was put on trial for rioting.

Many particulars are omitted, but it was proven by James Sanders, that said James Blankenship was rather the best looking young man of the whole family. The result was that Blankenship was cleared, and as soon as the verdict was read by the Clerk, Blankenship with hat in hand appeared, and in a loud voice thanked the jury, at the same time bowing quite low and giving his right foot a heavy scrape on the floor. The whole audience was immediately in a roar of laughter, even Judge Mason did smile audible himself.

The following particulars of his life is given as a warning to young men and as facts for temperance lecturers. Now let me

---

[124] Facial features
[125] Was selected and enrolled
[126] lengthy and complicated procedure
[127] premeditated and deliberate criminal act

preface this narrative by saying that I have been intimately acquainted with Blankenship for more than a third of a century. He had a wonderful memory thirty years ago, with a capacity to mimic that has seldom been excelled by our best actors; as a general thing he could repeat all the prominent points of some three or four stump speeches, all heard in one day, and some times make important and appropriate improvements. Some of these stump speeches were unique specimens of oratory, and I hope some specimens may have been preserved. In 1839, 1840 and 1841, be was about Bonaparte. Most of the old settlers will still remember him as a handy man at almost anything; could sing a song or tell an anecdote equal to any man. He was fond of liquor, but up to this time, at which he must have been thirty-one or thirty-two years of age, had control over his appetite for liquor. I had occasion to caution him a few times, but he replied he could always quit as pleased.

In 1843 he moved into Lee County, Iowa near Croton, and near the same time I moved to Sweet Home, Clark County, Missouri. Of course we were near neighbors again. About this time he used to go occasionally to Farmington for a spree[128].

His wife, Becky, was a great hand for pickled cucumbers, and prepared what was called whisky pickles. I believe they generally use about one gallon of whisky in making a barrel of pickles, but in Blankenship's family it generally took from five to seven gallons to make one barrel of pickles.

In 1845 the habit of drinking had grown on him so much that he reluctantly acknowledged to me that he could not always quit whenever he pleased, and in the fall of that year he had his first spell of delirium tremors. His sufferings were terrible.

About the year 1846 he moved over into Missouri some five miles from Athens, near Tom Caldwell's, His appetite for bad whisky by this time had almost complete control over him, so much so that he had several spells of delirium tremens, and

---

[128] random act of fun and sport with no direction

his sufferings were pitiable to behold. He not only had snakes in his boots, but they were all around and over him in his imagination coiling themselves all around him, occasionally taking two or three turns around his neck and choking him. Then legions of small devils would come, and with their tails throw darts into him, as porcupines are said to shoot their quills.

He suffered frequently in this way until about 1850, when he had a terrible spell, and was thought to have been dead by friends, and in his own imagination Old Lucifer came for him in his own proper person, but by some miraculous interference he was not allowed to take Jim at the time, but the devil removed a kind of veil from his face and gave him a full view of his Physiognomy[129], but it was his glowing eyes that fascinated Jim, he looked so long and earnestly waiting for the time that he might carry off James Blankenship bodily that after he recovered he picked up his little effects, and moved away up on Soap Creek, in Appanoose County, Iowa. That scare sobered Jim; he joined the Methodist Church, and remained perfectly sober for some four or five years, in which time he prayed regularly in his family, and gave frequent exhortations publicly.

Then he again moved back near Athens into the same cabin in which he lived when the devil came to him, but so long as Blankenship remained duly sober, the devil has not so much as called to see him.

Now I should like to know who will presume to say that whisky is not the devil?

After Blankenship had remained sober about six years, he came to solicit me to join the church, saying that my advice to him had been the means of reclaiming him, and now he wanted to be instrumental in my salvation. He admitted that the snakes and small devils might have been from liquor, but contended that the visit of Old Lucifer himself was no hallucination; that with him it was a fixed fact,

---

[129] facial features

incontrovertible[130]. I thought it might as well remain so with him, and ceased to argue the point.

About 1859 he moved to the State of Mississippi, near Natchez, took the care of some old people, and was inclined to be a Reb. during the war. He came into this neighborhood again in 1865, and the last that I knew of him he was living on the Missouri River not far from Arrow Rock, and I am afraid that he may yet commence drinking again.

Neither have I entire confidence in any man's religion that is scared into any church by an imaginary devil.

James Blankenship might have made a fortune on the theatre, or he might have made an eminent minister of the Gospel. As it is; he has only been drunken Jim Blankenship most of his life.

It was in the fall of 1834, and while at work building camp Des Moines, since known as Montrose, that I made the acquaintance of **William Bratten**.

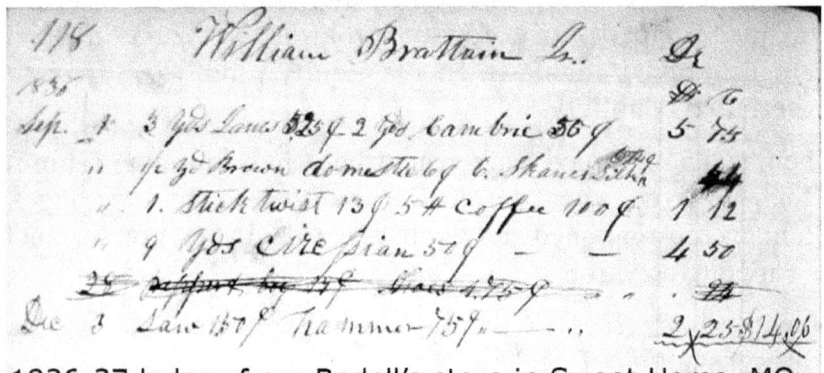

1836-37 ledger from Bedell's store in Sweet Home, MO

He was quite young at that time, perhaps not over twenty years of age; rather spare built, with a keen black eye, always kept his face, hands and, clothing neater than most other laborers, and could take a violin in hands quite gracefully, and play a tune called "Roarin' River" tolerable well.

---

[130] not able to be denied or disputed

From inquiry I learned that he lived somewhere below Warsaw, Ill, was poor and had been raised an orphan; although he had an uncle, Wm. Bratten, though his uncle had no means, if he had any disposition, to help him in any way.

William Bratten came on to the Des Moines in the fall of 1835, and in the summer of 1836, worked as hand keel boating or anything else he could find to do. I saw him frequently. He was gentlemanly in his demeanor[131], kept sober amongst a boats crew that dissipated considerably, and still kept his person uncommonly neat for one of his occupation.

He married rather young, and had a claim back in the suburbs of Farmington, lived very quietly, and took to reading history.

About December 1837, in passing through Farmington I had occasion to stay over night. There was a meeting of the debating club that night, and as usual, I took a part. In order to gain a point, I made some quotations from history rather carelessly or at random. William Bratten in following me used me up most completely, rectifying the quotations that I had made and gave some arguments that surprised me, in short, he literally annihilated me. I felt my defeat keenly, but had the grace to admire the industry and perseverance of my competitor in acquiring knowledge under difficulties.

I heard that he had moved up into Jefferson County, Iowa, and for some years lost the run of him, until about the year 1856. I received from Mr. Brawley, of Georgetown or Big Mound an invitation to come up and hear Mr. Bratten. An Universalist who was going to preach in that vicinity. On further inquiry I learned that it was my old friend. Now if I was writing biographies I would just have reached the interesting part, but as I am only writing sketches of early settlers on the Des Moines from my own knowledge, I must hold on, simply adding a word of encouragement to young men.

---

[131] Outward behavior or actions

The reader will please bear in mind that Wm. Bratten was raised an orphan boy on the extreme frontier of Illinois, was poor, had scarcely any opportunity for education, worked amongst about as rough a set of fellows as was ever on any frontier, yet he sustained himself honorably, and is to this day called the eloquent and learned Divine with all the more honor for having overcome such formidable difficulties.

Let young men that are despondent look at his success, take courage and do likewise.

And also, let the young man that finds himself the principle actor in scenes of hilarity and dissipation take warning by the result in the case of James Blankenship.

In the spring of 1835 **James Jordan**, an Indian trader, that had the previous winter occupied a trading house not far from the present location of Kilbourne on the D.V. Railroad, moved down on to a claim previously occupied by his brother Jeff Jordan on the opposite side of the Des Moines, from where the town of Bonaparte is now situated, about a mile and a half below the place, at this date, is owned by William Perkins, and I think he remained there until in 1838, he then moved to Iowa Falls, where he still resides and is, I believe, still able to answer roll call.

Mr Patchett settled in the spring of 1836 and afterwards became proprietor, with others, of the village of Philadelphia, another one of the almost extinct villages, being succeeded by the R. R. station called Kilbourne.

Mr. Patchett had a small corn patch in 1836, which I believe was the highest up the river of any settler, though the Indians had the same year considerable cornfields at Iowaville, and also back of Independence.

The last time I ever saw Mr. Patchett was in 1851, in the city of Sacramento, California. He said he took his whole family with him and expected to remain.

James Jenkins A single man and a cooper by trade, made a claim some distance above Patchett in 1836. Although he kept Bachelor's Hall, I do not think that he raised any corn that season. This Mr. James Jenkins was the first treasurer of Van Buren County, and for a year or two carried the treasury in his bell crowned hat.

He afterwards moved on the Fox River in Clark County, Missouri, where he remained some 5 or 6 years and then moved down on to the Mississippi bottom near Alexandria and must have died about the year 1846.

Edward L. Longwell came into the bend of the Des Moines River back from Keosauqua in 1837. He was a young man, with dark complexion, black hair and eyes, about five feet nine inches in height, stood erect, and was remarkably well muscled; in short, built up for endurance and action.

It was a custom with many of the first settlers in this section of country to take what they called a bee hunt in the Fall. Some four, five or six persons would associate together, take some breadstuffs, some feed, and four or five empty barrels, and go out west near the Indian lands in quest of honey. It was no uncommon occurrence to return within ten or twelve days with a full wagon load of honey.

During those bee hunts I have heard of the Indians ordering some few of the hunters off from their lands, but do not remember of their ever harming any one.

A party for a bee hunt was got up in Van Buren, now Keosauqua. It was composed of Meashack Sigler, Samuel Ragsdale, the Traveler Bill Smith, E.L. Longwell, and some others. This party, besides the empty barrels, took with them a two gallon jug full of American brandy, and went up the "Divide," as it was called at that time, and turned to the left, into Fox River timber, some five miles west of Troy, at present in Davis County.

There was no one of this company that was an experienced bee hunter and the weather was unfavorable, yet while the liquor lasted they all kept in spirits, but when the liquor gave out they began to despond.

Meashack Sigler and Samuel Ragsdale were fond of fun, as well as liquor. They managed to get Longwell and Smith and some one else to examine a tree on a certain place to see if there were any bees at work in the morning.

Bill Smith had his rifle. Longwell had no gun with him, while the other two were looking for bees where there were none. Sigler and Ragsdale disguised themselves as Indians and fired on them, not with a view to hurt them, but only to frighten them. The traveler, Bill Smith, jumped down a steep bank, running the muzzle of his gun into the mud about two feet, and left it sticking there whilst he crept into a tree top that was lying near by and hid himself like a young quail.

Longwell started to run for the camp. Sigler and Ragsdale, with blankets on, like Indians, run to head him off, when some one else, dressed as an Indian, appeared between them and the camp, and fired off a gun. Longwell, supposing the whole party would be killed, struck a bee-line for Keosauqua, and all hands testify that they had never, before or since, seen his speed excelled excepting by the race horse or Andrew McComb's dog. A very tall, yellow dog was with him at the start, trying to keep up, yelping occasionally and gradually falling behind, unable to keep up.

It was about 8 o'clock in the morning when Longwell started. About 10 o'clock he reached the place where Ellis & Mussetter were building their mill. He reported the rest of the party all killed, and he alone was left to bear the news to the settlements, having run about fourteen miles in two hours, most of the way over broken, brushy ground in north of Troy and down Chequest[132] timber.

At Ellis & Mussetter's mills he slackened his pace and reached Keosauqua a little after twelve. Here he again reported all the party as killed, he alone being left.

---

[132] Area east of Troy and North West of Keosauqua, Iowa

John Sigler fully believed the report and walked up and down the river bank boo-hooing just where Manning's store now stands, saying "Brother Mish is killed."

Longwell, after resting a few minutes, came on down to where Duncan and Wetherbee were building a mill; just where Kenneday's mill now stands at this place the writer hereof heard all the particulars from Longwell himself and am satisfied that he fully believed what he stated.

And I will now give the story just as he related it; after the firing as heretofore stated and seeing himself cut off from camp, he broke for the settlements; running his best licks for about three miles, he would hear McComb's dog behind yelping, he halted with a view of killing the dog to stop his noise, fearing that, the Indians would follow him by hearing the dog; on second thought, fearing delay might be dangerous, he kept on some two miles further, and running over a smooth piece of prairie, he looked back some distance, but could not see any Indians. The dog was still in sight yelping; he drew his knife from his belt with the intention of cutting his throat, but as the dog came up, he saw that his tongue was hanging out of his mouth, six inches. He knew that dog could not follow much further, so he spared him, and turning again he took his course at his best speed; in jumping ravines, he said, he could light just where he pleased; he also said in running rather down hill in Chequest brush he suddenly came on to a big Buck that started to run the course he wanted to go; that he placed his hand on his rump and rested himself a little while running, that the Buck did not go quite fast enough to suit him, neither did the Buck keep the exact course, so he just pushed him to one side and took the lead himself.

When he had finished his narrative, I told him that it was some of Meashack Sigler's devilment.

In a little while William McBride came down to see, what had best be done about the matter. I told him I was satisfied it was only some of Sigler's mischief. He was of the same opinion. But Sigler's wife was somewhat uneasy, and McBride and Elisha Buett run a few bullets, wiped up their rifles and started for the scene of the imaginary massacre, and just about where the little village of Lebanon now stands met the whole party coming home; and on enquiry, why they had acted so strangely, Sigler said the liquor give out and they felt a little dry and wanted a little amusement before starting for home. They all reached home a little after dusk.

A few words in explanation may be necessary. It is a well known fact among frontier settlers that some men, under the influence of a big scare, can perform wonderful feats of strength and agility, whilst others are unnerved and utterly powerless.

In this case Longwell experienced no farther inconvenience than having a wonderful appetite for a few days; and it might be as well to say the party that morning, at the time of the alarm, were five miles into the Indian's country, the boundary line being about half a mile above Troy at that date, September, 1838.

Glossary:

&c.	etc.
abate	retreat, subside, decline
about	in the vicinity of
acclivity	an upward slope
alderney	extinct breed of cow from a British Island
atone	make amends or reparation
bach	a small modest home (bachelor's crib)
bane	cause of great distress
batch	living as a bachelor
blarneying	using charm and pleasant flattery to persuade
bombast	high-sounding language- little meaning to impress people
caboose	small ship's kitchen
Campbellites	follower of Thomas Campbell – Disciples of Christ claim they originated from them.
carmine	deep-red pigment from the cochineal scale
chicanery	deception by sophisticated trickery
chide	scold or rebuke
clamor	loud confused shouting
compelled	force or oblige (someone) to do something
compunctions	feeling of guilt that follows doing something bad
corpulency	overweight
disconsolate	cheerless, unhappy
doggery	a cheap saloon
eddy	circular movement of water, causing whirlpool
edifying	providing moral or intellectual instruction

embark	begin a course of action
empanelled	enrolled the jury
enjoined	urged or instructed to do
epithets	descriptive phrase of personal characteristics
espoused	to support a cause
euphonious	pleasing to the ear
exultation	triumphant yell of joy
fisticuffs	fighting with the fists
flitters	bread cooked similar to pancakes
foray	raid or sudden attack
fourpence	British coin worth 1/60th of a pound sterling
freshet	spring thaw of the river
furore	outburst of enthusiasm or excitement
gullied	eroded ravine in soil
held sway	have a controlling interest
impetuous	quickly without thought or care
incontrovertible	not able to be denied or disputed
inculated	impress upon or teach by frequent instruction
Inkpaduta	Ink-pa-du-ta a chief of the Wahpekute band of the Dakota)
intimation	indication or hint
inveterate	long established habit
jorums	large jug or bowl for serving liquor
larrup	to beat or thrash
lawing	exercising the practice of law
leggings	buckskin leg coverings
linn	Wood from a linden or basswood tree
linsey	coarse woven fabric
lope	long bounding stride
lugubrious	Looking or sounding sad and dismal.
malice prepence	premeditated and deliberate criminal act
milch	Middle English for milk

nimrod	mighty hunter
panoply	splendid display
perfidious	deceitful and untrustworthy
Phiz	a persons face or expression
physiognomy	facial features
pickets	Soldiers performing a specific function
pugilistical	related to fist fighting
puncheon	split log with one face smoothed
reconnoitering	make a military observation
recreancy	shameful cowardice
rigmarole	lengthy and complicated procedure
rout	disorderly retreat of defeated troops
sallied	a military sortie - sudden rush
skullduggery	underhanded or unscrupulous behavior
slough	stagnant wetland, swamp, or shallow lake
sock-dolger	a forceful blow
succor	give assistance or aid
sutlers	civilian merchant who sells provisions to an army
temerity	excessive confidence or boldness, audacity
tow	coarse, broken fibre, removed during processing flax
vedettes	mounted sentry beyond outposts to observe enemy movements
verdue	Green growth health and vigor
wammus	heavy wool shirt
whit	a very small part or amount
wick-a-up	shelter made of sticks and bark
wight	unfortunate living human being

Definition of Indian Words and Names

Ah-ke-toh-koh-he-hoh	Chief Soldier
Ah-ki-to-ton-kah	Big Soldier
Ah-lo-wah	Running Over
ah-wi-pe-tuck	Head of the cascades or rapids.
Almo	half wolf indian dog
Cha-ha-nah-she	Standing Roof
Cha-her-ton-kah	Big Valley
Che-to-hoh	Buffalo Skin
Cocus	Hog
E-sa-wal-la	Mean
Fish	Water
Ghe-mans	Canoes
Goat	One
Goatawatso	Seven
Ha-e-she-stah	Twisted Horn
Hah-hah-sah	Grass Rope
He-sa-us-cuck	son of Black Hawk
Hi-o-kohe	Bare Leg
Hoh-sho-noh-she	Calico
Hon-no-pah-sa	Dark
Ho-wah-sop-pee	Black Fish
Hu-lah-he	Eagle Feathers
Hulan-shin-ka	Little Eagle
Igh-ho-was	Iowa Indians
In-co-ho-nec	Meaning the Great Father
Inkpaduta	Ink-pa-du-ta - war chief of the Wahpekute band of the Dakota
kah-kah-kaw	black hawk
Kah-wah-skin-koh	Little Horse
Keshuswe	the sun
linsey wammus	Linen hunting shirt
Mahaskah	white cloud
Mah-koh-shoot-sa	Red Medicine
Massages	rattle snakes

Mau-haw-gaw	Wounding Arrow- Chief
Maw-he-hum-no-che	the American big house
Me-kah-shin-koh	Little Coon
Me-kah-wah-she-a	Mad Coon
Me-kuh-hah	Coon Skin
Me-poh-hoh	Sun Rise
mishanoby papoose	a boy
Mis-so-rah-tar-ra-haw	female deer that bounds over the prairie
Moh-shob-ke-tah-skin-kah	"Little Soldier"
Moh-sho-ko-she	Distant Land':
Moh-shon-ko-she	Land Traveler
Muscoet-ipaw	Red Whiskers
nack-a-lo-ka-shees	best horse's
Nah-hoot-sa-in-ka	No Ears
napawnee	Flour
Nash-eas-kuk	Black Hawk's oldest son
Ne-kah-wah-she-ton-kah	Ambitious Man
Ne-koh-shoot-sa	Red Man
Ne-o-ho-neo	"Master of Rivers"
Neum	four
Neumnome	five
Noh-she-wah-tra-kah	Stand Easy
Non-sa-si-ka	Hard Heart
Nowatsocowatso	six
nucatucashaw	horse
O-koh-sha-pa	Twilight
O-koh-sho-moh-e	A Tumbler
Pah-her-cha-she	Shake Head
Pah-in-pah-tra	Bloated Pawnee
Pan-ne-no-pashe	Governor Joe's name
Pa-sha-ah-hoh	Yellow Stone
Pashepaho	Pash-e-pa-ho Stabbing Chief
Pau-hoo-chee	Original Iowas Name
Pe-she-ma-na-po	O.P. Thomas
Petete-ah-kah-kah-kaw	Little Black Sparrow
Pick-a-ninnies	small children

Po-to-won-ok	"fire place" or "chimney."
puch-e-she-tuck	the foot of cascade or rapids
Quick	nine
Rant-che-wai-me	Female Flying Pigeon
Scotch	fire
se-se-pawk-wah	sugar creek bottom
Sha-pa-tra-a	Big Soldier
Shaw	eight
She-se-pac	sugar
Sho-me-kob-se	Wolf
Shushkeses	young women
Sin-su-hoh-ha	Bright Tail
Skin-e-way	young man
Skon-ku-le-he	Scared Dog
Sno-qu	Rattlesnake
Sow-wow-wiskanoo	Yellow Bird
succotash	corn and beans
sway	three
Tah-bu-shin-ka	Little Hunter
Tah-ha-kah-ha	Horn Maker
Tah-wan-kah-ha	Town Maker
tom-i-noch	seed corn
Wah-a-tra koh-she	"Never Failed"
Wah-hoh-hoh	Lightning Bug
Wah-ho-tah-wah-no-she	"Take away Gun"
Wah-kon-te-ke	Doctor
Wah-le-gre-in-ka	"No Sense"
Wah-no-pah-she	Not Afraid
Wah-sha-hoot-sa	Grey Bird
Wah-tah-kone-lah	Want to Beg
Wah-toh-he-wa	Grey Mush
wish	Two

INDEX:

Alderney, 13
Alfrey, James, 101
Alfrey, Mrs., 101, 102
Anderson, Absalom, 36
Anson, Frank, 115
Anson, George, 115
Anson, Henry, 115
Avery, William, 87
Bailey, Dr., 135
Banditti of the Prairie, 126
Bateman, Henry, 137
battle, 80, 86, 87, 93, 118, 134
battle of Bad Ax, 59, 62
battle of Iowaville, 53, 54, 85
battle of Sink Hole, 72
Beach, Mr., 85
Bears, 32
Bedell, Mrs Nancy, 14
bees, 146
Benton, Thomas H., 39
Bentonsport, 117
Berquinn, Leiut., 110
Big Island groves, 91
Bird, Isaac, 138
blacksmith, 29
Blankenship, James, 138, 140, 141, 142, 144
Blankenship, Thomas, 134, 138
Brand, Father, 26
brandy, 145
Bratten, William, 109, 142, 143
Brawley, Mr., 143
Bride, 20, 30
Bronthes, 112
Brown, Captain, 110
Buett, Elisha, 147
Buffalo, 15, 76, 92
Burgess, Rev. John, 17
Burkholder, Mr., 96
Burner, Mr., 121
Burtis place, 109
Butcher, 31, 32
CA, Sacramento, 144
cabin, 19, 30, 59, 60, 70, 72, 121, 141
caboose, 26
Caldwell, Tom, 140
California, 9, 107, 118, 126, 127, 138
Campbellite, 21, 23
Canada, British Columbia, 118

canoe, 77
Carr, Brother, 18
Carr, Dick, 36, 38, 39
Cartwright, Rev. Barton H., 25
Chambers, Gov., 65
Charlton, Thomas, 131
Cheney, Dick, 8
Church Baptist, 18, 19, 22, 23, 58, 103
Church Methodist, 48, 127, 134
Church Presbyterian, Bluestocking, 23
Church Universalist, 143
Church, Francis, 117
Church, Mrs., 93
Clark, Billy, 11, 14
Clarke, Adam, 47
Clay, Henry, 63, 64
Cleghorn & Harrison, 50
Colwell, Tom, 14
Connable, A.L., 50
Creel, Mr., 26
Crossman, Lieut. G.H., 108, 112
devil, 57, 111, 141, 142
Dodd Store, 27
Dodd, Orrin, 27
Dodd, Warren, 27
dog, 122, 135, 146, 147
doggery, 27
Dragoons, 15, 108, 110
Driscoll, Mr., 27
Duncan, Mr., 147
Elbert, Dr. J.D., 124
Ellis & Mussetter, 146
Ely, David A., 116
Fallis, William, 138
fight, 26, 37, 54, 72, 79, 81, 82, 103, 113, 117
Fleak, L.B, 50
Forquaen, Captain, 114
Freshet, 12, 31
Galland, Abel, 104, 105
Galland, Dr. Isaac, 5, 6, 9
Garber, C., 50
Gardner, Miss, 99
Gaston, Charles, 135
Gillis, Peter, 115
Goodwin, John, 116
GRIMES, JAMES W., 91
grist mill, 132

ix

guard, 84, 99
Gunsmith, 29
Hairy Breasted warrior, 106
half-breed, 93, 97
Hamill, Smith, 50
Harlan, A.W., 14, 114
Haywood, George, 14
Hearn, Samuel, 13, 14
Hefferman, Henry, 128
Helm, Bill, 138
Higgins, Brother, 18
Hinder, John, 32
Hitt, Daniel, 48
Hog, 3, 24, 33, 69, 112
Howell, J.B., 49
Humphrey, D.A., 50
IA Territory, 124, 133, 138, 139
IA, Agency, 14
IA, Alexandria, 47
IA, Appanoose Co., 141
IA, Atlantic, 44
IA, Bentonsport, 12, 71, 114, 116, 118, 134, 137, 138
IA, Birmingham, 29, 69
IA, Black Hawk, 30
IA, Bloomington, 24
IA, Bonaparte, 30, 65, 120, 131, 133, 134, 136, 137, 140, 144
IA, Burlington, 6, 25, 65, 67
IA, Camp Des Moines, 8, 55, 108, 112
IA, Cass Co., 44
IA, Charleston, 26, 42
IA, Chequest, 146, 147
IA, Clay Co., 94
IA, Council Bluffs, 15, 44, 105, 106
IA, Croton, 53, 140
IA, Davis Co., 63, 145
IA, Des Moines, 14
IA, Devil Creek, 8, 55, 56, 57, 58, 59, 77
IA, Dickinson Co., 94, 95
IA, Dubuque, 5, 15, 24, 108
IA, Eddyville, 41
IA, Emmitt Co., 91, 94
IA, Fairfield, 42
IA, Farmington, 136, 140, 143
IA, Flint Hills, 6
IA, Fort Madison, 6, 8, 9, 26, 59, 61, 77
IA, Fort Sanford, 14
IA, Fox River, 145

IA, Georgetown, 143
IA, Independence, 144
IA, Independent, 78
IA, Indian Creek, 121
IA, Iowaville, 30, 37, 63, 67, 69, 73, 78, 144
IA, Jefferson Co., 104, 143
IA, Keosauqua, 25, 29, 30, 49, 50, 115, 121, 124, 125, 135, 139, 145, 146
IA, Lebanon, 48, 148
IA, Lee Co., 9, 11, 53, 62, 63, 108, 140
IA, Lexington, 30, 65, 136, 137, 138
IA, Libertyville, 42
IA, Louisa Co., 28
IA, Monticello, 117
IA, Montrose, 8, 9, 53, 54, 108, 112, 116, 125, 126, 142
IA, Muscatine, 24
IA, Nashville, 11
IA, Philadelphia, 29, 30, 144
IA, Pittsburg, 123, 124
IA, Pottawattamie Co., 44
IA, Raccoon Forks, 14
IA, Richmond, 74
IA, Rising Sun, 123
IA, Rochester, 30
IA, Rock Creek, 115
IA, Troy, 145, 146, 148
IA, Utica, 47, 50
IA, Van Buren Co., 30, 47, 53, 65, 107, 108, 123, 124, 128, 131, 133, 139, 145
IA, Vernon, 135
IA, Wapello Co., 67
IA, Zarahemla, 9
IL, Fort Clark, 11
IL, Galena, 5, 11, 106, 108
IL, Hancock Co., 112, 117
IL, Montrose, 74
IL, Nauvoo, 8, 9, 77, 125
IL, Quincy, 65
IL, Rock Island, 6, 62
IL, Rock River, 73, 76, 77
IL, Warsaw, 54, 143
Illinois, 24, 56, 74, 105, 137, 144
IN, Brookville, 11
IN, Wabash, 111
Indian Trader, 71, 106, 144
Jackson, Mr., 30
Jenkins, James, 144
Johnson, Captain, 96

Johnstone, Captain, 95
Jones, Richard M., 104
Jordan, James, 144
Kearney, Col., 110
Keith, Isham, 133
Keith, Thomas, 133
Kenneday, John, 26, 27, 147
Kentucky, 26, 27, 101, 116, 134, 136
Knapp, Nathaniel, 8
KY, Green River, 118
LA, New Orleans, 127
Lawton, Jacob, 29
liquor, 72, 82, 110, 140, 141, 145, 146, 148
Longwell, Edward L., 145
Lowe, Gov., 99, 100
Lucas, Gov., 28, 65
Manning Store, 147
MAP-1839 SE Iowa, 16
MAP-Bentonsport, d
MAP-SE Iowa, j
MAP-Territory, i
Martin, Captain, 100
Mason, Charles, 139
Mason, Judge, 27, 139
Mattock, Esq., 97
Maxwell, Jo, 135
Maxwell, Lieut., 95
Maxwell, Samuel, 135
McBride, William, 147
McCarty, Dr. Isaac, 115
McComb, Andrew, 146
Meek Family, 30
Meek, Robert, 131
Meek, Wm. Jr., 132
Meek, Wm. Sr., 131, 132, 133
MI, Beaver Island, 105
MI, Lake Michigan, 105
Michigan, 110, 131
Miller, Captain, 50
Minnesota, 35, 38, 73
Mississippi, 142
Mississippi River, 5, 24, 36, 38, 53, 54, 73, 77, 110, 116, 145
Missouri, 11, 30, 39, 101, 103, 105, 110, 118, 134, 137, 140
Missouri Frontier, 72
Missouri River, 35, 85, 97, 142
MN, Ft..Ridgely, 93, 95
MN, St. Paul, 38, 47
MO, Alexandria, 31, 145
MO, Arrow Rock, 142
MO, Athens, 14, 140, 141
MO, Clark Co., 11, 73, 140, 145
MO, Fox River, 145
MO, Independence, 111
MO, Lancaster, 118
MO, Lincoln Co., 73
MO, Palmyra, 120
MO, Ralls Co., 104
MO, Schuyler Co., 118
MO, St. Charles, 36, 38
MO, St. Francisville, 11, 12, 14
MO, St. Louis, 32, 39, 47, 73, 109, 116
MO, Sweet Home, 13, 140
MO, Waterloo, 121
Moffatt, John, 131
Moffatt, Robert, 131
Morgan, Captain, 15
Mormon, 9, 105, 106, 125, 126
Morrison, Mr., 97
MS, Natchez, 142
Musick, Lewis, 36, 37, 38
NAI Chief Black Hawk, 5, 8, 9, 53, 54, 55, 59, 60, 61, 62, 63, 64, 65, 67, 69, 72, 73, 74, 76, 78, 79, 80, 84, 85, 86, 88, 134
NAI Chief Black Hawk, Madam, 61, 62
NAI Chief Hardfish, 63, 85
NAI Chief Keokuk, 60, 62, 63, 67, 85, 87
NAI Chief Wapello, 62, 63
NAI Chippewa, 37
NAI Comanche, 120
NAI Fox and Sauk, 53, 73, 76, 79, 81, 85
NAI Indian, 75, 80, 81, 83, 91, 96, 111, 145, 146, 148
NAI Inkpaduta, 99, 100
NAI Iowa Indians, 53, 54, 73, 75, 76, 78, 79, 80, 81, 84, 85, 87, 88
NAI Monemonees, 73
NAI Nauasia, 61
NAI Nes-se-as-kuk, 60
NAI Pashepaho, 53, 54, 72, 73, 74, 78, 79, 80, 82, 83, 84, 85, 87
NAI Pe-she-ma-na-po, 72
NAI Pottawattamie, 69
NAI Sioux, 37, 73, 91, 94, 95, 96, 97
NAI Winnebago, 73

xi

NAL arrow, 75, 80
NAL Best Horses, 76
NAL Braves, 37, 74, 76, 78, 81, 84, 85, 87, 88
NAL keshuswe, the Sun, 84
NAL Muscoet-ipaw, 72, 116
NAL Scouts, 75, 80
NAL she-se-pac, 56, 75
NAL Shushkese, 88
NAL skin-e-way, 76, 88
NAL Sow-Sow-wiskanoo, 72
NAL Squaw, 8, 59, 75, 93, 94
NAL tomahawk, 6, 78, 79, 82, 83, 84, 87
NAL wammus, 19
NC, Raleigh, 103
ND, Pembina, 35
Nelson, Morton, 119
Netherton, Henry, 87
Nixon, Squire, 50
North Carolina, 103
Nottoway, 55
Nowell, Mr., 121, 122
NY, Greene Co., 126
Old Baggy, 103
Overhall, Ezra, 110
Patchett, Mr., 144
Perkins, Joseph, 135
Perkins, William, 144
Petri, John, 107
Phelps, Bill, 13, 14
Phillips, John, 11, 13
plow, 1
Plummer, Henry, 72, 114, 121, 122
Points, John, 25, 26
Powel, James, 114
prairie, 12, 36, 38, 41, 43, 44, 45, 63, 76, 78, 79, 80, 83, 84, 88, 92, 96, 116, 133, 147
Pratt, Seth, 115
President, 100
President Jackson, 64
Purdom, Elijah, 115
quail, 45, 146
Ragsdale, Samuel, 145, 146
Railroad, 25, 36, 44, 144
Ratlan, Hamp, 25
Reed, Mr., 62
Reid, Col. J.M., 31
Reid, Isaac, 135, 136, 137
Reid, Samuel C., 114, 119

Richards, Captain, 97
Ross, Shapley P., 117, 120
sale, 24, 103, 137
Saloon, 27
Salty Sam, 119
Sample, Hugh W., 50
Sanders, James, 114, 120, 134, 139
Sanford, Charles O., 117
scalps, 74, 75, 78, 79, 81, 82, 83, 84, 85, 88
Scottish, 35
scouts, 92
Selkirk, Lord, 35, 36, 39
Sheldon, Mr., 112
Sheriff, 104, 128
Sigler, John, 147
Sigler, Meashack, 145
Skunk, 88
Slaughter, John, 114
slavery, 3, 4, 117
Smith, Bill, 145, 146
soldier, 6, 88, 109, 110, 112, 122
Solomon, Mr., 26
Spencer, John, 48
steamboat, 127, 132
Steel, James, 29
stranger, 113, 134, 136
stream, 13, 17, 38, 82, 91, 92
Sullivan, Giles O., 36, 55, 71, 72, 78, 86, 87, 109, 110, 112, 114, 116, 117, 120, 135, 137
Sullivan, Winnena, 118
Sweasey, Hazen, 109
temperance, 23, 28, 139
Tennessee, 27
Territorial Council, 124
Texas, 13, 117, 118, 120, 122, 138
Thomas, O.P., 72, 114
Tilvers, John, 115
TN, McMinn Co., 133
Tollses, 127
Toole, 28
Trabue, Dr., 11
Trading House, Caboo, 93
Turner, Dr., 65
Valley, 11
Vannoy, 115
vedettes, 78, 80, 82, 84
venison, 75, 77, 105
Vinson, Malachi, 48
Virginia, 26, 138

Virginian, 106
wagon, 1, 3, 31, 47, 50, 92, 96, 121, 145
Washburn, Mrs., 43
Wayland, Jerry, 11, 12, 14
Wetherbee, Mr., 147
wheelwright, 29
White, Captain James, 108, 112, 113, 114
WI Territory, 24, 119, 121
WI, Green Bay, 73, 126, 127
Wick-a-up, 55, 59, 60, 61, 63

Willcock, David, 120
Williams, Abiatha B., 123, 124, 125, 126, 127, 128, 129
Williams, Barent A., 126, 128, 129
Willis, Thomas, 117
Willis, Winnena, 117
Wilson, Mr., 8
withes, 1
wood, 1, 2, 47, 57, 70, 88, 138
woods, 17, 47, 77, 82
Yankee, 23, 24, 26, 29, 39

NOTES:

www.ingramcontent.com/pod-product-compliance
Lightning Source LLC
Chambersburg PA
CBHW050538300426
44113CB00012B/2160